HIEROGLYPHS WITHOUT MYSTERY

HIEROGLYPHS WITHOUT MYSTERY

AN INTRODUCTION TO ANCIENT EGYPTIAN WRITING

Karl-Theodor Zauzich

Translated and Adapted for
English-Speaking Readers
by Ann Macy Roth

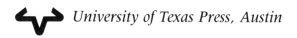 *University of Texas Press, Austin*

Cover adapted from design by Gerhard R. Hauptmann, Berlin.
Explanation of the text appears in Section 3.13.

Library of Congress Cataloging-in-Publication Data

Zauzich, Karl-Theodor.
    [Hieroglyphen ohne Geheimnis. English]
    Hieroglyphs without mystery : an introduction to ancient Egyptian
    writing / by Karl-Theodor Zauzich ; translated and adapted for
    English-speaking readers by Ann Macy Roth. — 1st ed.
        p.   cm.
    Translation of: Hieroglyphen ohne Geheimnis.
    Includes bibliographical references.
    ISBN 0-292-79804-0 (pbk.)
    1. Egyptian language—Writing, Hieroglyphic.   I. Roth, Ann Macy,
    1954–   . II. Title.
    PJ1097.Z38   1992
    493'.1—dc20   91-47600

First published by Verlag Philipp von Zabern, Mainz, as
HIEROGLYPHEN OHNE GEHEIMNIS
© Verlag Philipp von Zabern 1980.

Table of Contents

Foreword   vii

Translator's Preface   ix

1. Generalities   1
1.1. Not for Geniuses Only   1
1.2. Beauty as a Rule for Spelling   2
1.3. Pictures but Not Picture Writing   4
1.4. How Egyptologists Speak Egyptian   6
1.5. What Is Transliteration?   9

2. The Writing System   11
2.1. The Egyptian Alphabet   11
2.2. Biliteral Signs   17
2.3. The Phonetic Complement   22
2.4. Triliteral Signs   23
2.5. Ideograms (Sense-Signs)   24
2.6. Determinatives   26
2.7. Graphic Peculiarities and Abbreviations   29
2.8. Complication and Simplification   34
2.9. A Little Grammar   35
     2.9.1. Grammatical Gender   35
     2.9.2. The Plural and the Dual   36
     2.9.3. Genitive Constructions   38
     2.9.4. Suffix Pronouns   39
     2.9.5. Adjectives   42

3. Examples   **44**
3.1.   An Architrave of Sahure   44
3.2.   A Glazed Tile from the Palace of
       Ramesses II at Qantir   47
3.3.   Lintel from a Temple or Palace of Ramesses II 50
3.4.   Fragment of a Tomb Wall   53
3.5.   A Wooden Box from the Treasures of
       Tutankhamun   55
3.6.   Tutankhamun's Alabaster Chest   59
3.7.   The Alabaster Cup of Tutankhamun   65
3.8.   A Canopic Coffin of Tutankhamun   67
3.9.   The Canopic Chest of Tutankhamun   70
3.10. Vignette from a Book of the Dead   74
3.11. The False Door of Khut-en-Ptah   81
3.12. The Tomb Stela of Tashep-Khonsu   85
3.13. The Hieroglyphs on the Cover: A Temple
       Inscription   88

4. Conclusion   **91**
4.1. Selected Royal Names   91
4.2. Names of Gods   93
4.3. Further Study of Hieroglyphs   95

5. Appendixes   **98**
5.1. Solutions to the Problems   98
5.2. Books on Egyptian Vocabulary and Grammar 101
5.3. Hieroglyphic Sign List   103
5.4. Museum Numbers and Photo Credits for
      the Objects Discussed   120

FOREWORD

What do all those hieroglyphs say? This question, which almost everyone who is interested in Egyptian art asks at one time or another, will be answered in this book. The basic principles of Egyptian hieroglyphic writing are probably much simpler than you imagine. In a few hours, you can learn these principles and then go on to read and understand simple inscriptions like the ones illustrated in the following pages. In the process, you will gain a new understanding of one of the oldest human civilizations—one that is in many ways related to our own. Since Jean François Champollion deciphered them in 1822, hieroglyphs have not been a mystery to scholars; now you too can penetrate their secrets.

TRANSLATOR'S PREFACE

Most people who are interested in the history, art, and society of ancient Egypt are curious about the hieroglyphs that have been sprinkled so liberally over its buildings, artwork, and artifacts. They suspect, quite correctly, that these little pictures would enrich their understanding and appreciation, if they could only read them. Unfortunately, the level of general knowledge about hieroglyphs that would be useful to an interested tourist or museum visitor is not easy to acquire.

The most popular books on Egyptian writing are simple explanations of the alphabet and signs for children. More sophisticated books describe the language and offer a daunting array of information on the decipherment of hieroglyphs, the development of other Egyptian scripts, and grammatical principles, but they devote little, if any, space to reading actual texts. Some ambitious amateurs will attempt to teach themselves to read hieroglyphs with the standard textbook, Sir Alan Gardiner's *Egyptian Grammar*. This is hard work and often yields only meager rewards. Most of Gardiner's examples and exercises are taken from stories and narratives, so that serious students can study the intricacies of Egyptian sentence structure. Few monumental texts are discussed. As a result, quite simple texts on monuments sometimes baffle students with a year or more of study behind them because their patterns and conventions are unfamiliar.

None of these books stresses the most intriguing feature of Egyptian hieroglyphs, which is that they are pictures. Hieroglyphs should not be separated from the scenes and buildings they label or the plants, animals, and objects they depict. The ancient Egyptians were just as fascinated by the pictorial character of hieroglyphic signs as we are today. Great lovers of puns and double meanings, the ancient scribes delighted in reinforcing and even extending the meaning of their words by the placement and details of the pictures they used to write their sounds. Properly understood, these ingenious plays on words and pictures illuminate Egyptian art and offer fascinating glimpses into the religious beliefs and cultural values of one of our earliest civilizations.

Professor Zauzich's *Hieroglyphen ohne Geheimnis* aims to inspire an appreciation of such nuances. It teaches the basic grammar and vocabulary needed to read most short inscriptions on monuments and artifacts, but it also stresses the relationships between the hieroglyphic signs and the subtle meanings these relationships convey. Moreover, the book gives abundant examples of the kinds of texts that tourists or museum visitors will encounter most frequently. Each text is fully explained, so that the reader will learn the general patterns and how to apply them to similar texts. The vocabulary is limited to the most frequently used words. Occasional questions, answered in the back of the book, allow the reader to work out some of the problems independently.

Most of the examples are taken from German museums and the Tutankhamun exhibition, but they all represent types of texts found in most Egyptian collections. The cover text alone (analyzed on p. 88) offers a prototype that will explain thousands of texts in temples all over Egypt. The readers who work their way through the examples given here may not be able to translate every inscription they encounter, but they will recognize the most common phrases and many of the names of kings and gods. More important, however, they will appreciate the rich religious symbolism and sophistication hidden in the seemingly naïve columns of birds, bees, and baskets that embellish Egyptian monuments.

One principal drawback to the book, that it has until now been available only in German and Dutch, will, I hope, be remedied by the present translation. In addition to more basic explanations of the grammatical forms that do not occur in English, this edition contains added linguistic and cultural references of special interest to English speakers; I hope that they are not so American as to be incomprehensible to speakers of other dialects. I have completely rewritten Section 4.3,

"Further Study of Hieroglyphs" and Section 5.2, "Books on Egyptian Vocabulary and Grammar," for English-speaking readers. If I have not always been able to resist the translator's temptation to make the text "better than it was before" (to quote an ancient Egyptian copyist), I hope at least not to have made it worse.

I am immeasurably indebted to my own teachers, Professors Edward F. Wente, Janet H. Johnson, and the late Klaus Baer, for introducing me to the twists and turns of ancient Egyptian grammar. I would also like to thank Robert Ritner and Everett Rowson for their comments on earlier drafts and to express my gratitude to the students in my courses in hieroglyphs at the American Research Center in Egypt and Tufts University's Experimental College for helping to point out the sticky places. Finally, I am grateful to Professor Zauzich for writing the book and for allowing me the pleasure of translating it. I hope that his English-speaking readers find this version as satisfying and enlightening as his German-speaking readers found the original.

HIEROGLYPHS WITHOUT MYSTERY

1. GENERALITIES

1.1. Not for Geniuses Only

This is the first point to remember: Egyptian hiero-glyphic writing was mastered in its own time by many people, most of whom were no more geniuses than present-day people (or Egyptologists) are. The writing system was, of course, slightly more complicated than our simple alphabetic system: our alphabet has twenty-six letters, while the Egyptian writing system of the Middle Kingdom contained about seven hundred signs (no one has counted them exactly), which could sometimes have more than one meaning. The beginner might find this rather intimidating, but the situation is not as bad as it sounds. Many of these signs are recognizable pictures with obvious meanings that do not need to be memorized. This book introduces roughly 150 hieroglyphs, which can be used to read many short inscriptions. Actually, not even Egyptologists need to memorize all the signs and their meanings, since rare signs can always be looked up in reference books.

Although there were many ancient Egyptians who could read and write, the relative complexity of the writing system ensured that there were many more who could not. Professional scribes were necessary, and to be a good scribe required years of study. Many of the homework assignments and classroom exercises written by those diligent students are today treasured as precious relics by the museums of the world. The mistakes they made in their exercises, interestingly, allow us to deduce that Egyptian writing was taught by the whole-word method rather than phonetically.

In one respect, however, Egyptian students had it easier than their modern counterparts: there are no strict spelling rules in Egyptian writing. In the place of spelling stood aesthetics.

1.2. Beauty as a Rule for Spelling

Whatever spelling looks right is correct. How happy modern students would be with this rule! Actually, aesthetic considerations are almost the only limit to the different ways in which hieroglyphic texts can be written, and that includes even the direction of the writing. Hieroglyphs could be written and read from right to left or from left to right, depending on where they were used. The individual signs were always turned so that they looked the reader in the face, and so that in reading them the viewer's eye passed over them from front to back. This is true of all hieroglyphs, but it is easier to see in the case of signs with human and animal forms. These always look toward the beginning of the line: if a line of writing is to be read from right to left, they look toward the right.

To give an illustration, if an inscription was carved around a doorway, the individual signs of the text would face in the direction of the arrows on the diagram. This allows a person walking through the door to read them most easily, since each text begins with the signs closest to the reader, and no sign is so "impolite" as to turn its back. Compare the "false door" pictured on p. 80.

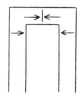

The placement of hieroglyphs in relation to one another was also governed by aesthetic rules. The Egyptians always tried to group signs in balanced rectangles. For example, the word for "health" was written with the three consonants s-n-b. These would not be written ㄴ~~ᐧ by an Egyptian; because the group would look ugly, it would be considered "incorrect." The "correct" writing would be the grouping of the signs into a rectangle ᐧ~~ᐧ . Compare the plate on p. 45.

The artistry with which the Egyptians constructed these rectangles can be seen in all the inscriptions in this book. The labor of construction was lightened some-

what by the fact that individual hieroglyphs could be
enlarged or shrunk as the grouping required, and that
some signs could be placed either horizontally or vertically (like the hieroglyph for the rolled document,
which could be either ⧲ or ⚊). Scribes would
even reverse the order of signs, if it seemed that a more
balanced rectangle could be obtained by writing them
in the wrong order.

As a result, many Egyptian words could be written
in two or more different ways; every writing was as
good as the next as long as the aesthetic rules were
followed (compare pp. 73 and 101).

Please note: In this book, hieroglyphs are written
to face right (so that the direction of reading is from
right to left, the opposite of English). This is because the
Egyptians always wrote from right to left when there
was no reason to choose one direction over another.
When an original text with left-facing hieroglyphs is
discussed, the orientation will be retained in our copy
and emphasized by an arrow (←), because there was
always some special reason for writing in this direction.

1.3. Pictures but Not Picture Writing

The ornamental charm of hieroglyphs lies in the fact
that each of the individual signs is a picture, which

the Egyptians frequently rendered in beautiful detail.
Almost all hieroglyphs represent either a living plant
or animal or a piece of equipment, and in most cases
they are not difficult to recognize. Since the signs are
not merely abstract geometric shapes, they are also
generally easy to learn, although many of them are
not at all easy to write. Don't be disappointed if the
first hieroglyphs you attempt to draw are less than
beautiful—it is only a question of practice.

Although hieroglyphic signs are pictures, hieroglyphic writing was not a "picture writing" in the true
sense, where the picture and its meaning are always
the same. The sign 🦉 , for example, does not usually
mean "owl," but rather the letter *m*. Between the pictorial sign 🦉 and the (apparently!) abstract geometric Latin letter *M* there is, in principle, no difference:
both are arbitrary signs representing the sound *m*. But
the matter is a bit more complicated, since many hieroglyphs could represent a sound in one context, while
in other places they had their original pictorial meaning. When a hieroglyph actually meant what it pictured, a short stroke, called a determinative stroke,
was added. For example, the hieroglyph ⬭ generally is to be read as the letter *r*; with the determinative
stroke ⬭̣ the same sign has the meaning "mouth"
or "speech."

Egyptian hieroglyphic writing is true picture writing,

with agreement between the picture and its meaning, only in a very limited way. This fact is basic to understanding the system. Before Champollion's brilliant
discovery of this fact in 1822, early scholars worked for
decades under the mistaken assumption that each hieroglyph had a symbolic meaning. As a result, all their
attempts at decipherment were in vain.

1.4. How Egyptologists Speak Egyptian

Nowhere among all the hieroglyphs is there a single
sign that represents the sound of a vowel. Egyptian
writing is thus a purely consonantal system, like
"unpointed" Hebrew or Arabic. Naturally, a string of
nothing but consonants can only be pronounced by
someone who knows which vowels belong in the
framework. This is less complicated than it sounds.
For example, any of us can read an advertisement that
consists almost entirely of consonants:

> 3rd flr apt in hse, 4 lg rms, exclnt loc nr cntr, prkg,
> w-b-frpl, hdwd flrs, skylts, ldry, $600 incl ht.

In the same way, an Arab can read a text in Arabic even when the vowels are not indicated by marks
over or under the consonants they are attached to. And

in the same way, an ancient Egyptian could read a hiero-glyphic text with the proper vowels, even though the vowels were not written. Through their familiarity with the appropriate language, each would know exactly which vowels fit into the framework of consonants.

But this poses a problem for Egyptologists: since the language written with hieroglyphs has been a dead language for almost two thousand years, no one knows exactly how ancient Egyptian words sounded. Philo-logical studies have, of course, allowed us to approxi-mate the vocalization of many words, but that is almost a separate science in itself. For everyday conversation, Egyptologists have adopted a simple, though rather drastic, rule to make the jumble of consonants pro-nounceable: they insert an *e* between each consonant. A word like *snb* is thus pronounced "seneb," the word *nfrt* is pronounced "neferet," and so forth. In addition, it has been agreed to pronounce certain consonants that have some vowel-like qualities as *a*, *i*, and *u* (see p. 13). The pronunciation that results from these con-ventions is, naturally, totally artificial. It is probably so far from the true pronunciation that an ancient Egyptian who heard a modern Egyptologist speaking "Egyptian" would find it impossible to understand, despite the fact that the two could communicate almost effortlessly in writing.

Admittedly, words using only the vowel *e* do not

have a particularly attractive sound. For this reason, other pronunciations that do not follow these rules have long been used for many royal names. Thus, the king's name that would be vocalized Imenhetep by Egyptological convention occurs in the literature as Amenhotep, Amunhotpe, Amenhetep, and so on. For the queen's name that would be vocalized Neferet-iiti, English speakers usually say Nefertiti, while Germans say Nofretete. Naturally, neither form is "correct"; the contemporary pronunciation of the name was most probably something like Nafteta, according to the most recent research.[1] Out of curiosity, someone once took the trouble to count all of the renditions in modern publications of the name *ʾIi-m-ḥtp*, who was the chief architect of King Djoser: he found thirty-four different forms.[2]

To complete the student's confusion, some kings' names also have Greek forms, known from classical authors, which are often used in modern books. As an example, the name Amenhotep was written by the Greeks as Amenophis. (For further examples, see pp. 91–93.) These Greek names can usually be recognized by their endings, which are *-os*, *-is*, or *-es*.

1. G. Fecht, *Zeitschrift für ägyptische Sprache und Altertumskunde* 85 (1960), 89.
2. J. B. Hurry, *Imhotep*. London: Oxford University Press, Oxford 1928, pp. 190ff.

1.5. What Is Transliteration?

In language studies and even in everyday life, it is
sometimes necessary to write foreign words and names
in our own script, so that a reader who does not know
the foreign script will have some idea of how the word
sounds. This process is called *transliteration*. Certain
conventional rules exist for setting down the individual
signs. Since different languages consist of different collections of sounds, it is not always simply a matter of
replacing each sign in one language with a single sign
in the other. More often, a single sign must be replaced
by a combination of signs or by signs with special dots
or strokes (called *diacritics*) added to them to show that
they have a different phonetic value. So, for example,
we transliterate a Greek *θ* as *th*, a Russian щ as *shch* or
šč, an Arabic ط as *ṭ*, and so forth.

In the same way, Egyptian hieroglyphic writing can
be transliterated. The rules for doing this are based on
convention, like all such rules, and these conventions
are not entirely consistent worldwide. Normally, only
the signs that have a sound value appear in transliltera-
tion. The silent signs that are used to clarify the meaning are left out.

A slightly different process is called *transcription*. In
English, this term is used when a text written in another Egyptian script is rewritten in hieroglyphs. The
process is like transliteration, except that both writing

systems are Egyptian. The most common use of transcription is to convert texts written in a cursive script called *hieratic* (see p. 79) into hieroglyphs. This process is rather like writing out someone's signature in block capital letters.

The Egyptian language used a number of sounds that do not occur in English. (This will be explained in detail in the next chapter.) Although vowels were not used, hieroglyphic writing was in some cases more complete in reproducing consonants than our alphabet can be, since it had a sign to stand for the "glottal stop," which occurs in English but is not written. A glottal stop is the consonantal sound that comes before a vowel at the beginning of a word if it is carefully pronounced: "I didn't say some mice, I said some *ice*." This consonant is used twice in the exclamation "uh oh!" and in some dialects of English as a substitute for a *t*, for example, the Cockney version of the phrase "a li(tt)le bo(tt)le." The glottal stop in Egyptian was written with the sign 𓄿 (letter name: aleph, transliteration: ꜣ). Another sound, which is not used in English at all, was written ꜥ (letter name: ayin, transliteration: ꜥ). It is a scratchy sound, even deeper in the throat, and can be approximated by imitating the sinister sound of a door slowly squeaking open. Aleph and ayin are actually consonants, but most Western Egyptologists pronounce them as an open *a*, as in f*a*ther.

2. THE WRITING SYSTEM

2.1. The Egyptian Alphabet

The Egyptians had an alphabet of twenty-four consonants. These signs are the first thing to learn.

Hieroglyph	Picture	Trans-literation	Pronunciation
	Egyptian vulture	ꜣ	a (aleph)
	reed leaf	ỉ	i or y
	double reed leaf	y	i or y
	lower arm	ꜥ	a (ayin)
	quail chick	w	w or u
	leg	b	b
	wicker stool	p	p
	viper	f	f
	owl	m	m
	water	n	n
	mouth	r	r
	courtyard (plan)	h	h

Hieroglyph	Picture	Trans-literation	Pronunciation
𓎛	twisted flax wick	*ḥ*	h (emphatic h)³
⊜	placenta(?)	*ḫ*	k (soft kh: German *ich*)
⟃𓈓	animal belly	*ẖ*	k (hard kh: German *ach*)
—₩—	door bolt	*z*	z
⎾	folded cloth	*s*	s
⊏⊐	pool	*š*	sh
△	sandy slope	*ḳ*	k (q without u: *qaf*)
⌒	basket	*k*	k
⊍	jar stand	*g*	g
◠	bread loaf	*t*	t
⊂•	tether rope	*ṯ*	ch
⊂◠	hand	*d*	d
ʃ	cobra	*ḏ*	j

3. In the English text of this book, this sound will be written ḫ.

Hieroglyph	Picture	Trans-literation	Pronunciation

Some Alternate Forms:

Hieroglyph	Picture	Trans-literation	Pronunciation
〃	two strokes	*y*	i or y
⭗	red crown	*n*	n
⭲	?	*m*	m
𓏲	from the cursive form	*w*	w

(The parenthetical pronunciations give a closer approximation of some of the non-English sounds that may be familiar to you if you know German, Hebrew, or Arabic. The reason for the differences between the transliteration and the sound of the letter in English is that most of these equivalents are used internationally.)

It is a good idea to memorize this group of hieroglyphs, as they are among the most common signs used. Practice drawing them, too; that will make it easier to remember them. Try to write your name in hieroglyphs. For vowels, use the following consonantal signs: 𓄿 for *a*; 𓇋 , 𓇌 , or 〃 for *i*, 𓅱 or 𓏲 for *o* and *u*. Short *e* and other unstressed vowels may be left out; if *e* occurs in a stressed syllable, use an ꜣ or an *i* or a *u*, whichever is closest. For example, Ben might be written simply *Bn*, while Eugene might

be written *Ywdîn*. For the *v* sound, use an *f*, since
Egyptian had no letter *v*; and for the *1*, you can use
the sign ⟨sign⟩ , which will be discussed below (see
p. 19). (In this exercise, you are in fact transliterating
your name into Egyptian, and transliterations are often
only approximate renditions of the original.) Try to
write the name as it sounds, not as we spell it with our
illogical historical spellings.

At the end of a masculine name, you should draw
the seated man sign ⟨sign⟩ ; at the end of a feminine
name, draw a seated woman, ⟨sign⟩ . Both signs are examples of another type of sign, called a *determinative*
(see p. 26).

Be sure that your hieroglyphs are always arranged
into tidy rectangles, as in the following names:

Can you read all these names? If not, you will find the solutions on p. 98.

The last name in the right column is actually taken from an ancient inscription. This shows that our technique for writing a non-Egyptian name in hieroglyphs is not a new one: it is borrowed from the Egyptians themselves, who used these rules whenever they had to write the name of a foreigner; for example, the names of their Greek rulers Cleopatra, Ptolemy (Ptolemaios), or Alexander (Alexandros).[4]

In principle, it would be possible to write every word in the Egyptian language with these few alphabetic signs. Unfortunately for the student of the language, the Egyptians were not satisfied with just these signs and usually used other kinds of signs as well. These will be explained in the next chapters. Nevertheless, some of the most common words were written only with alphabetic signs, and it will be useful to learn a few of them at this point.

Writing	Trans- literation	Pronun- ciation	Meaning
〰	*n*	en	to, for (preposition)
𓅓	*m*	em	in, from, as (preposition)

---

4. The last name in the left column is also an ancient writing, except that the final *s* (for the Greek ending *-os*) was left off.

Writing	Trans-literation	Pronunciation	Meaning
or	*ỉn*	in	by (preposition of agent)
	ḫr	ker	with, near (preposition)
	nty	nety	which (relative pronoun)
	snb	seneb	health
	twt [5]	tut	picture, image
	Zrḳ.t [6]	Serket	(the goddess) Selket
	Ptḥ	Peteḥ [7]	(the god) Ptah
	Rˁ [5]	Ra [7]	(the god) Re
	p.t [5, 6]	pet	heaven, sky
	ḫ.t [5, 6]	ket	thing, matter, property
	ỉrp [5]	irep	wine
	ḏ.t [5, 6]	jet	eternity

5. The last sign is silent. These signs will be explained on p. 26.

6. The period can be ignored for now. It will be explained on p. 36.

7. This is the pronunciation called for by the rules given above; however, Egyptologists often pronounce the names of gods differently, using pronunciations that have become established in the field and that are usually based on the forms used by classical authors. Instead of Pe-teḥ, one usually says Ptah; instead of Ra, Re; and for Imen, Amon or Amun. See also p. 93.

2.2. Biliteral Signs

It may well be asked why the Egyptians developed a complicated writing system that used several hundred signs when they could have used their alphabet of thirty signs and made their language much easier to read and write. This puzzling fact probably has a historical explanation: the one-consonant signs were not "discovered" until after the other signs were in use. Since by that time the entire writing system was established, it could not be discarded, for specific religious reasons. Hieroglyphs were regarded as a precious gift of Thoth, the god of wisdom. To stop using many of these signs and to change the entire system of writing would have been considered both a sacrilege and an immense loss, not to mention the fact that such a change would make all the older texts meaningless at a single blow. Given this religious importance, it makes sense that the complicated hieroglyphic writing system was only abandoned when the Egyptians converted to a new religion, Christianity.

In addition to alphabetic signs (consisting of one consonant each), Egyptian writing had four other categories of hieroglyphs. The first of these are the biliteral signs, which, as the name suggests, represent a combination of two letters (consonants). Of the approximately one hundred signs of this type, about thirty are given here. They, too, should be memorized eventually.

Biliteral Sign			Transliteration	Egyptological Pronunciation
⧤			ꜥꜣ	aa
⧸			wꜣ	wa
⧹	and	⧺	pꜣ	pa
⧻			mꜣ	ma
⧼			ḥꜣ	ḥa
⧽			ḫꜣ	kha
⧾			zꜣ	za
⧿			šꜣ	sha
⨀			kꜣ	ka
—	and	⨁	tꜣ	ta
⨂			ḏꜣ	ja
⨃			mỉ	mi
⨄			tỉ	ti
⨅	and	⨆	dỉ	di
⨇			ḫꜥ	kha
⨈			ꜣw	aw
⨉			nw	nu

Biliteral Sign			Transliteration	Egyptological Pronunciation
☌			rw^8	ru
↓			sw	su
▽			nb	neb
⚶			ḥp	ḥep
⊍			ḥm	ḥem
⊐⫙			tm	tem
⊂⊐			ỉn	in
⬳			wn	wen
⊔			mn	men
⌇	and	↓	sn	sen
⊶			ỉr	ir
⬱			wr	wer
⊏⊐			pr	per
⊅	and	⊏⊥	mr	mer
♀			ḥr	ḥer

8. This sign was frequently used to approximate the sound *l* in rendering non-Egyptian words in hieroglyphs.

Biliteral Sign	Transliteration	Egyptological Pronunciation
𓐍	*ẖr*	kher
𓁈	*ms*	mes
𓋴	*ḥḏ*	ḥej

Like the alphabetic signs, all biliteral signs can be used in completely unrelated words. For example:

𓇓	*sw.t*	sut "sedge plant" (the heraldic plant of Upper Egypt). The stroke (a determinative stroke) indicates that the hieroglyph represents here exactly what it pictures. The *t* at the end is the ending of a feminine word (see p. 36) and is separated from the stem of the word by a period.
𓄿	*H̱nsw*	Khonsu (the moon god)
𓇓	*n-sw.t*	nesut "king of Upper Egypt." The word is to be read this way despite the actual order of the hieroglyphs (*sw-t-n*). See p. 31.

In the following examples of the use of the biliteral sign *k3*, each word ends with a silent sign, like the seated man or seated woman that follows a personal name. These signs, called *determinatives*, are more fully explained beginning on p. 26.

𓃓 𓂓	*k₃*	ka "bull"
𓀀 𓂓	*k₃.t*	kat "work"
𓆏 𓂓	*k₃m*	kam "vineyard"

Many biliteral signs can also be independent words, occurring alone or with a determinative stroke (see p. 5) or a suitable determinative. For example:

∝	*ꜥ₃*	great, large
𓅨	*wr*	great
𓅭	*z₃*	son
▽	*nb*	all, any, every
🏠	*pr*	house
👁	*ỉr*	do, make
🜂	*mr*	love
⚘	*ḥr*	upon, on account of
𓂓	*k₃*	ka (an untranslatable religious concept, meaning something like a person's immortal soul)

2.3. The Phonetic Complement

Hidden behind this technical-sounding term is help for
those who are worried by the number of biliteral signs.
Not to be confused with a compli*m*ent, these "sound
completers" make learning and reading hieroglyphic
signs much simpler. Phonetic complements are alphabetic signs (the same ones you have already learned)
that are added after a multiconsonantal sign to clarify
it. Instead of writing the group *sw* as , for example,
it is often written , as though it were to be read
sw-w. However, the correct reading is still *sw*, because
the additional *w*, the phonetic complement, is only a
hint to the reader. Often both consonants in a biliteral
sign are "doubled" by phonetic complements in this
way: for example, ꜥꜣ "great" (written as if it
were ꜥꜣ-ꜥ-ꜣ).

There are no hard-and-fast rules for the use of phonetic complements. Certain groups of signs tended to
be used, more or less predictably, in individual words.
Here as well, the criterion seemed to be whether the
signs used could be grouped into aesthetically pleasing
rectangles. The name of the god Amun was almost always written with a final *n* as a phonetic complement:
 , that is, *ỉ-mn-n*, to be read *ỉmn*, and pronounced
by Egyptologists as Imen or (more commonly) Amun
or Amon (see note 7, p. 16).

Try to decipher the following kings' names, which are written exclusively with phonetic signs. (Solutions are on p. 98.)

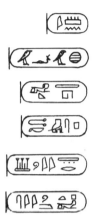

2.4. Triliteral Signs

Triliteral signs, as their name suggests, represent three letters (consonants). They are similar in principle to the biliteral signs, but naturally they are much rarer. Only a few need to be memorized now, along with the meanings that they very often have when they stand alone:

𓆣	*ḫpr*	become, happen
𓄤	*nfr*	beauty, be beautiful

⌀	*ḥtp*	be satisfied, peaceful
⌁	*stp*	select, choose
⌂	*ḫrw*	voice
⌟ or ⌐ or ⌠	*ḫnt*	in front of, foremost
⌡	*s3ḥ*	approach, draw near

Triliteral signs may also be provided with phonetic complements, for example:

⌬	*ḫpr*	(written as *ḫpr-r*)
⌭	*nfr*	(written as *nfr-f-r*)

2.5. Ideograms (Sense-Signs)

The three types of hieroglyphs dealt with so far resemble each other in that they represent certain sounds or combinations of sounds, and in that they can be used in words of very different meanings. They are, in other words, sound-signs, in which there is no necessary connection between the picture and its meaning.

By contrast, ideograms (sense-signs) can stand for whole words or concepts. Used this way, they can also be called *logograms* (word-signs). As an indication that these hieroglyphs mean what they picture, a small stroke is added to them, for example:

⚹	*sb̲ꜣ*	"star"
♡	*ỉb*	"heart"
🐝	*bỉ.t*	"bee" (the *t* is the ending of a feminine word)
⊙	*r ᶜ*	"sun"
⌐	*nt̲r*	"god"

The number of logograms in Egyptian script is quite large. Some of the most common will appear in the following readings and examples. Many of them are easy to recognize, even for a reader not used to Egyptian artistic conventions. But for other signs, like the logogram for *nt̲r* "god," a thorough knowledge of Egyptian culture lies behind the connection of the sign to its meaning.

Logograms also are frequently supplied with phonetic complements. The word "star" occurs in the following writings:

⚹ *s-b-sb̲ꜣ*

⚹ *s-b-ꜣ-sb̲ꜣ*

In either case, only *sb̲ꜣ* (Egyptological pronunciation: seba) is to be read. Out of examples like this one there may have developed another use of ideograms, which will be discussed in the next section.

2.6. Determinatives

Determinatives can also be seen as a kind of ideogram. They invariably stand at the end of a word, and, in contrast to all of the signs introduced so far, they are silent. Their task is to indicate the range of meaning in which a word belongs. Because of their position at the end of a word, they also serve as word dividers, since there are no spaces between words in hieroglyphic writing. A few examples will illustrate the use of determinatives.

At the end of words for people are written a seated man ⟨glyph⟩ or a seated woman ⟨glyph⟩ :

⟨glyph⟩	*it*	"father" (the third sign, *f*, is silent in this word)
⟨glyph⟩	*ḥm.t*	"wife"
⟨glyph⟩	*nb*	"lord"
⟨glyph⟩	*nb.t*	"lady," "mistress"

If the word includes both men and women, a seated man and a seated woman are written with a group of three strokes that indicate a plural:

⟨glyph⟩	*mhw.t*	"family"

Behind verbs that describe motion, small running legs are written as a determinative:

△ 🖵   *pr*   "go forth"

If the motion is in a backward direction, that is also shown in the determinative:

△ ⌐⌐ ᨖ   *ʿn*   "turn back, return"

Words that have to do with force and exertion are often written with the striking man:

𓀜 𓂝 𓍁 𓏲𓏭   *sk₃*   "plow"

This last example shows that two (or more) determinatives—here a plow and the striking man—can be included in the same word.

Most determinatives are easy to memorize, because they are so intuitively obvious, as in

𓀜𓏲𓍁𓏤   *i₃w*   "old man"

𓀜𓏙𓍢𓏭   *shdhd*   "be stood on one's head"

Perhaps you can discover for yourself what the determinatives attached to some of the words in the list beginning on p. 16 mean. Some, though not all, should be easy to recognize. (The meanings are given on p. 98.)

The choice of certain determinatives often says something about the opinions of the ancient author. When he writes the word for "education" with the striking man sign, it throws a rather suspicious light on the pedagogical methods of his time. When the same determinative is used after the word for "taxes," it becomes almost a political statement.

But the most valuable role of determinatives is to distinguish words that would otherwise be identical. In a language with no vowels, many words with very different meanings can be written with the same signs. We need only imagine what would happen if there were no vowels in English. How would we know whether the word *sl* was to be read *seal*, or *soul*, or *aisle*, or *sly*, or *sale*, or even *Oslo*? Only the context, or an additional sign that indicated the approximate range of meaning of the word, could help us decide. That is exactly what determinatives do, as the following examples will show. Here are six words that all have the same pair of consonants *wn* (pronounced wen) and their meanings:

    "open"   determinative: a door

"hurry"   determinative: running legs

🐦〰️	"mistake"	determinative: small bird written with bad and small things, called the "evil bird" by Egyptologists
🪶〰️	"become bald"	determinative: a lock of hair
⊗〰️	"Hermo-polis"	determinative: a city with crossed roads
☀〰️	"light"	determinative: the sun with rays

The cartouche ⬭ , which surrounded royal names, can also be understood as a kind of determinative.

2.7. Graphic Peculiarities and Abbreviations

The Egyptians never thought of their script as simply an arbitrary, mechanical method of communication. It also had the religious and magical power to bless or to curse, during this life and on into the life after death. Many inscriptions, especially those on temple and tomb walls, were intended "for eternity." Under such circumstances, who would not take special care with their forms? But the goal of this care was not only aesthetic beauty (such as the balanced rectangles discussed on pp. 3–4), but also the meaningful arrangement of the parts of a text to convey an intellectual connection. As one example of this, on the alabaster cup of Tutankhamun (see p. 64), the royal name is oriented to the right, while the words "beloved of Amun . . ." are oriented to the left, so that the signs in the two texts face each other, literally representing by their arrangement the love between the god and the king. This can hardly be a coincidence, since thousands of similar examples prove that the turning was intentional (see also p. 51).

Another scribal custom with a religious explanation creates difficulties in the reading of royal names and many names of private individuals. Such names usually consist of several words and frequently form a complete sentence. Normally, one of the components is the name of a god or goddess, for example, "Amun is satisfied" (= Amenhotep) or "Re has given him birth" (= Ramesses). But in order to honor the divinity mentioned, the divine name was written at the beginning, even if grammatically it belonged in another place. This happened not only in names of people, but in names of places, in titles, and in certain formulas. Instead of Tut-ankh-Amun (= "Living image of Amun"), the name was written Amun-tut-ankh (p. 57); instead of Sahure (= "One whom Re nears"), Re-sahu was written (p. 44); instead of Ankhes-en-Amun (= "She lives for Amun"), Amun-ankhes-en was written (p. 62);

and so forth. The correct reading of royal and private
names in which gods' names occur can only be deter-
mined by someone with a thorough knowledge of the
Egyptian language, and even then the readings are not
always certain, since Egyptologists themselves differ
over how some names should be read. (For further
examples of royal names, see p. 91.)

Not only were the names of gods moved forward,
but also the general word for god, ⌐ *ntr*, was shown
the same respect in some composite expressions. Three
examples of these writings are:

it-ntr "father of the god, god's father" (a priestly title):
⌐ ⌐⌐ . This common title can also occur in abbreviated forms, such as ⌐⌐ or ⌐⌐ (p. 78).

hr.t-ntr "gods' land" = "necropolis" (cemetery): ⌐⌐⌐
(p. 79). If these signs are not familiar, they can be looked
up in the sign list beginning on p. 103 under R8, T28, D21,
X1, and N25.

s-ntr "incense" ⌐⌐⌐ (p. 55) or ⌐⌐⌐ (p. 87).
Can you explain all the signs of both writings? If not,
you will find a brief clarification on p. 99.

The same inversion used with the word *ntr* also
occurs in expressions that contain the word "king." This
word itself contains an inversion, for we read ⌐⌐

"king [of Upper Egypt]" not as *sw.t-n* but as *n-sw.t*; the
sedge plant has been moved to the front of the word
since it serves as a royal emblem. Correspondingly, the
title of noble women "acquaintance of the king" *rḫ.t-
nsw.t* is not written ⟨glyph⟩, but ⟨glyph⟩ , which
looks like *(n)sw.t-rḫ.t* (see p. 82).[9] In the same way, the
Egyptians wrote the titles "noblewoman of the king"
šps.t-nsw.t as ⟨glyph⟩ (p. 82) and "wife of the king" (or
"queen") as ⟨glyph⟩ *ḥm.t-nsw.t* (p. 62).

This is also the place to discuss the formula with
which most prayers to the dead on steles and other
monuments begin: ⟨glyph⟩ or ⟨glyph⟩ and variants.
It is to be read *ḥtp-dỉ-nsw.t* (Egyptological pronunciation "ḥetep-di-nesut"), although it is usually written
either *(n)sw.t-dỉ-ḥtp* or *(n)sw.t-ḥtp-dỉ*, as in the examples
discussed on pp. 78, 81, and 87.

The translation of this ancient formula as "an offering that the king gives" is a bit problematic, since
the meaning evolved over the centuries of its use;
however, we cannot examine these questions more
closely here.

Some of the very common expressions used in mor-
tuary cults are usually written in abbreviated form.

---

9. The function and meaning of this title, which has been much
discussed in the Egyptological literature, will not be dealt with here.

Among them is the name of the offering itself:
pr.t-(r)-ḥrw, literally "the going forth at the voice"
(meaning the voice of the person who is saying the
prayer and making the offering for the soul of the dead
person). This is usually written ⟨glyph⟩ . You already
know the first two signs of these four; the others are
explained in the sign list beginning p. 103 under O3.

A dead man is commonly called ⟨glyph⟩ *im3ḥw*
and a dead woman ⟨glyph⟩ *im3ḥw.t*, meaning "honored" or "venerated." Another epithet given the dead
person is ⟨glyph⟩ *m3ꜥ-ḥrw*, literally "true of voice," im-
plying that the person has been judged innocent in the
court of the dead. It is put at the end of the deceased's
name and is frequently abbreviated ⟨glyph⟩ or even
more briefly ⟨glyph⟩ (see p. 85) or ⟨glyph⟩ . Sometimes all or
part of this group is written reversed, so that it faces
the name of the deceased (see p. 70).

It should also be mentioned here that deceased
people of both sexes could also be addressed as "Osiris." The Egyptians hoped to become one with this god
after death, and this title demonstrates their belief that
this unification had taken place.

Another important abbreviation is ⟨glyph⟩ , which appears very frequently on temple walls and elsewhere.
It introduces words that are meant to be the speech of
a god. The abbreviation is to be read as *ḏd mdw*, meaning "words spoken" or "words to be spoken," and is

often followed by the phrase "by god (or goddess) X"
(see pp. 69 and 89). In many cases these two signs
have a function similar to our quotation marks: they
introduce direct speech.

One final abbreviation should be mentioned, which
is often written behind kings' names: ⌐⍾⊤ . It consists
of the triliteral sign *ʿnḫ* as a writing for *ʿnḫ* "life," the
biliteral sign *ḏꜣ* as an abbreviation for *wḏꜣ* "prosperity,"
and the alphabetic sign *s* as an abbreviation for *snb*
"health." "Life, prosperity, and health!" are good wishes
for the king; may they also be granted to all those who
have worked their way this far through the book.

2.8. Complication and Simplification

The hieroglyphic system thus consists of two large
groups of signs: sound-signs (phonograms) and sense-
signs (ideograms). The phonograms can be further
divided into alphabetic, biliteral, and triliteral signs,
while the ideograms are either logograms, standing
for the sound and meaning of a whole word, or silent
determinatives:

Unfortunately, this simple theoretical explanation is complicated by the fact that most hieroglyphs vary in function, appearing sometimes as phonograms, sometimes as logograms, and sometimes as determinatives. In some cases the function of a hieroglyph is so nebulous that professional Egyptologists disagree about which category it should be assigned to.

But there is no need to be discouraged by the complications of theoretical categories, because luckily they have relatively little bearing on the actual reading of hieroglyphic texts. In the following examples, there is no need to determine whether a given hieroglyph is, for example, a biliteral or a logogram. It is enough to know how it should be read and what it means. If you have forgotten how to read a sign, you can always look it up in the sign list beginning on p. 103.

2.9. A Little Grammar

Before going on to read short inscriptions, it is necessary to introduce a few rules of grammar, without which the texts will not make sense. Don't worry; there are only a very few.

2.9.1. Grammatical Gender

In Egyptian, as in most languages other than English, nouns that have nothing to do with men or women have grammatical gender. All nouns are either masculine or feminine and are referred back to by the pronouns "he" or "she." (Egyptian has no real "it," or neuter gender.) Masculine and feminine words are usually easy to distinguish in Egyptian, because feminine words have a *t* as an ending. In transliteration, endings such as this are divided by a period from the stem of the word, for example:

	nb	lord		*nb.t*	lady, mistress
	sn	brother		*sn.t*	sister
	pr	house		*nh.t*	sycamore tree

Some verbs also take a feminine ending when they form infinitives (nouns expressing verbal action), for example, *ir.t* "to do" or "to make." The *.t* of the feminine ending often is not written, however. *Warning*: Not every *t* at the end of a word is a feminine ending!

2.9.2. The Plural and the Dual
The ending of the plural (masculine *.w*, feminine *.wt*) usually is not spelled out phonetically but is shown graphically. Plurality can be expressed in three different ways:

With three strokes

⌷⌷⌷   *pr.w*   houses   ⌐P   *nṯr.w*   gods

With three little circles (only in certain words)

⦂⌐   *db.w*   figs

By tripling a logogram or a determinative

⌷⌷⌷   *pr.w*   houses   ΓΓΓ   *nṯr.w*   gods

ᙡᙡᙡ   *ns.wt*   thrones   ◊◊◊   *nh.wt* sycamore trees

For pairs of things, Egyptian has a separate form, the dual, which is shown in a similar manner. The dual endings are *.wy* (masculine) and *.ty* (feminine); they are normally shown by doubling the sign.

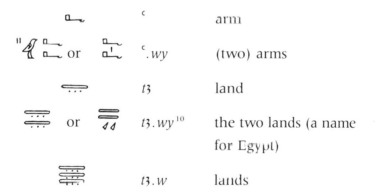

⍽	ꜥ	arm	
ꜥꜥ or ꜥꜥ	ꜥ.wy	(two) arms	
⎓	t3	land	
⎓⎓ or ⎓⎓	t3.wy[10]	the two lands (a name for Egypt)	
⎓⎓⎓	t3.w	lands	

10. The land-sign is often written without its dots or with an additional determinative (sign list N21); see p. 66.

2.9.3. *Genitive Constructions*

A genitive construction is a way of connecting two nouns, which we do in English by using "of" or the possessive ending "'s." The Egyptians also expressed the genitive in two ways: either directly, by juxtaposition of the two connected nouns, or indirectly, by the use of the genitive particle ⚊ *n* "of." In the examples in this book, the direct genitive is most common:

	nb.t pr	mistress of the house (p. 86)
	nb p.t	lord of heaven (or "heaven's lord") (p. 66)
	nb ẖ͘.w	lord of crowns (p. 59)
	nsw.t nṯr.w	king of the gods (p. 78)
	z3 Rᶜ	son of Re (or "Re's son") (p. 47)
	3w ỉb	wideness of heart (= happy) (p. 46)

The indirect genitive is even more straightforward:

	r3 n z	the mouth of a man (p. 79)

2.9.4. Suffix Pronouns

A suffix is a short word that is attached to the end of other words. Egyptian contains a very common set of suffixes that correspond to our personal pronouns I, you, she, and so forth. Only a few of them need to be learned here, namely,

$=i$	I
$=k$	you (said to a man)
$=f$	he
$=s$	she

In transliteration, suffixes are divided from the words they are attached to by an equal-sign. In hieroglyphs they are written with the appropriate alphabetic signs (p. 11), which are ⌒ , ⟶ , and ⌐ . During the period dealt with in this book, however, the first-person, singular suffix $=i$ ("I") was not written with the reed leaf ⌐ , as might be expected. Instead the appropriate personal determinative was used:

𓀀	if the writer or speaker was a man
𓁐	if the writer or speaker was a woman
𓀭	if the writer or speaker was a god

Warning: In many cases the first-person, singular suffix is not written at all and has to be supplied from the context.

The function of these suffixes depends on the nature of the word to which they are attached.

1. Attached to a noun, a suffix shows possession:

𓊃𓈖	*sn*	brother
𓊃𓈖	*sn=k*	your brother
𓂓	*k3=k*	your ka (p. 66)
𓄣	*ib=f*	his heart (p. 46)

2. Attached to a verb, a suffix forms the so-called *sḏm=f* conjugation:

𓂞	*di=k*	you give
𓁹	*ir=f*	he makes
𓋹	*ꜥnḫ=s*	she lives

These verbal forms are called *sḏm=f* forms (pronounced sejemef) in Egyptian grammar, after the pattern verb *sḏm*, "hear." In most of the examples in this book, including those above, they are translated as an English present tense. Although this is not technically correct (the Egyptian indication of tenses is actually

quite complex), the present tense is the simplest way
to approximate the meaning of *sḏm=f* forms. In some
cases they can also express a wish, as in

$$\text{[hieroglyph]} \quad \textit{dỉ=f} \qquad \text{may he give (p. 78)}$$

Which of these two translations for a *sḏm=f* form is
appropriate in a given place often simply depends on
the context.

In these sentences, the suffix functions as the sub-
ject. A noun, of course, can also serve this function,
and it is also placed directly after the verb:

$$\text{[hieroglyph]} \quad \textit{ʿnḫ=k} \qquad \text{you live (or may you live)}$$

$$\text{[hieroglyph]} \quad \textit{ʿnḫ k}ꜣ \qquad \text{the ka lives (or may the ka live)}$$

$$\text{[hieroglyph]} \quad \textit{ʿnḫ k}ꜣ\textit{=k} \qquad \text{your ka lives (or may your ka live)}$$
$$\qquad\qquad\qquad\qquad\qquad\qquad \text{(p. 66)}$$

3. Attached to a verb plus *n*, a suffix forms the *sḏm-
n=f*.

If an *n* is placed between a verb and a suffix pronoun, a past tense is formed, which is called a *sḏm-n=f*
form (pronounced sejemenef), again after the pattern
verb *sḏm*; for example,

$$\text{[hieroglyph]} \quad \textit{ỉr-n=k} \qquad \text{you have made}$$

$$\text{[hieroglyph]} \quad \textit{dỉ-n=ỉ} \qquad \text{I have given (said by a woman)}$$

4. Attached to a preposition, a suffix serves as the object of the preposition. With *n*, for example,

~~ ◯	*n=k*	for you
~~ ⌐	*n=f*	to him
~~ ▭▵ ⌐ ~~~	*dỉ-n(=ỉ)* *n=f*	I have given to him (see p. 40 for the omission of the suffix = ỉ)

When a suffix is attached to the preposition 𓍯 *m* "in," it takes a fuller form, 𓇋𓅓 *ỉm*, as in

𓀀 𓇋𓅓	*ỉm=ỉ*	in me
𓇋𓅓	*ỉm=k*	in you
𓏤 𓇋𓅓	*ỉm=s*	in her

When an object rather than a person is referred back to, the gender of the suffix pronoun used to refer back to it must be the same as the grammatical gender of the noun. For example, referring back to a house (*pr*, which is masculine), the Egyptians wrote *ỉm=f* "in it" (literally, "in him"); to refer back to a sycamore tree (*nh.t*, which is feminine), they wrote *n=s* "of it" (literally, "of her").

2.9.5. Adjectives

Adjectives, which describe nouns just as in English, have the same number and gender as the nouns they

are describing. As a rule, however, an adjective is written *after* the noun.

𓊹𓄤	*nṯr nfr*	the good god (i.e., the king)
𓐍𓏏𓎟𓏏	*ḫ.t nb.t*	every thing

The Egyptian language can make adjectives out of
prepositions by adding the ending *-y* (or *-y.t* in the
feminine); for example,

𓏃	*ḥr*	upon
𓏃	*ḥry*	high, highest
𓏃	*ḫnt*	in front of
𓏃	*ḫnty*	foremost, first

The ending is very frequently left unwritten; see,
for example, *ḫnt(y)* "first" on p. 82.

3. EXAMPLES

3.1. An Architrave of Sahure

The first inscription to be studied is inscribed on an architrave that stood over a doorway in the temple of King Sahure (about 2450 B.C.) and that is now on display in the Egyptian Museum in Berlin. The finely balanced composition of the signs, which are carved in very hard red granite, is a wonder in itself. As the grid laid over the photo shows, the text fits into rectangular boxes, equal in width almost to the millimeter, yet the effect of the text is neither stiff nor constrained on that account, perhaps because the spacing between the boxes is varied. There are, incidentally, other proportions and alignments in the text that are certainly not coincidental—perhaps you can find them yourself. One hint: the diagonals of the second box cross exactly in the center of the sun-sign.

    Now for the text itself. The first box, which is only partly preserved, contained a royal title "the golden Horus," which will not be explained further here. Boxes 2 and 3, which are surrounded by the cartouche (see p. 29), give the name of the king. The first sign of this is the logogram of the sun, to be read R^c (see p. 25). The second hieroglyph is the triliteral sign for $s3ḥ$; therefore, the complete cartouche has the signs R^c-$s3ḥ$-w, which can be understood as $S3ḥ$-w-R^c, according to

the rules explained on p. 30, and pronounced Saḥure.
The name might be translated as "he to whom Re
draws near."

The rest of the text on the architrave contains good
wishes for the king. In the fourth box are three logograms: the looped cross, or "ankh" sign, ꜥnḫ "life";
the pillar *ḏd* "stability"; and the scepter *wꜣs* "dominion." Box 5 is the word *snb* "health," written with alphabetic signs only. The next box contains the wish
for "happiness," written with the biliteral (or logogram) *ꜣw* "wide"; the logogram *ỉb* "heart"; and the
alphabetic sign *f*, the suffix "his." Together then we
have *ꜣw ỉb=f*, literally "May his heart be wide" (see
p. 38).

The last box holds the word "eternity" or "forever." It is written with two alphabetic signs (*ḏ.t*) and
the usual determinative of this word, the flat land sign.
Perhaps you already know this word if you like im-
ported cookies: a German cookie company has taken
this group as a trademark, along with the slightly
erroneous transliteration TET. Apparently, the cookies
will keep forever.

The entire inscription, after the damaged section,
may be transliterated *Sꜣḥw-R* ꜥ *ꜥnḫ ḏd wꜣs snb ꜣw-ỉb=f
ḏ.t* and translated "Sahure, life, stability, dominion,
health, and happiness forever."

A twin of this architrave in the same museum bears
exactly the same text running in the opposite direction,

but it is more badly damaged than the architrave shown here.

3.2. A Glazed Tile from the Palace of Ramesses II at Qantir

At the time of their accession to the throne, all Egyptian kings adopted an official royal *titulary*, a set of honorific names introduced by a standard sequence of royal titles. In its fullest form, this titulary consisted of five names, each of which had a special function and meaning. The most important and most frequently used of these were the two names written in cartouches: the praenomen introduced by the title ⚘⚘ *(n)sw.t-bỉ.t* "king of Upper and Lower Egypt"[11] and the nomen introduced by the title ⚘ *z3-Rᶜ* "son of Re." The nomen was, as a rule, the name of the king before he became king—in other words, his personal name or birth name. The additional names taken at the coronation sometimes embodied references to specific religious and political programs, just as the names chosen by popes sometimes do today, but these references are for the most part only rarely and partially detectable. Our understanding of the statements made in royal

---

11. The title *(n)sw.t-bỉ.t* means literally "the one who belongs to the sedge plant [the heraldic symbol for Upper Egypt] and to the bee [a heraldic symbol for Lower Egypt]."

names is still very unsatisfactory, primarily because it is never certain which of the translations that are grammatically possible for each name is correct.

On the blue faience tile pictured here, the *(n)sw.t-bỉ.t* name of Ramesses II (1290–1224 B.C.) is inlaid in Egyptian alabaster. The individual hieroglyphs are

← ☉	sun		logogram: the god Re
	jackal head		triliteral *wsr*, here a short form of the word *wsr* "be strong"
	goddess with a feather		logogram: the goddess of justice, Maat (*M3ˁt*), who carries the sign ˁ*nḫ*, "life"
	adze on a block of wood		triliteral *stp*, here a short form of the word *stp* "choose"
〜〜	water		alphabetic sign *n*

The name of the sun god Re occurs twice in this royal name, and in both cases it has been moved forward to honor the god (see p. 30), so that the signs are to be read *Wsr-m3ˁ.t-Rˁ-stp-n-Rˁ* (pronounced Usermaatre-setepenre). The first part of this name, incidentally, is the original form of the name Ozymandias, the title of Shelley's poem about the ruined statues of the Ramesseum temple in Luxor, which includes the lines:

"My name is Ozymandias, king of kings:
Look on my works, ye Mighty, and despair!"

The translation of the compound name Usermaatre-
setepenre is very uncertain, for the reason given above.
It is usually interpreted as "the Maat of Re is strong [a
sḏm=f form of *wsr*; see p. 40], one chosen [a parti-
ciple, or adjective form, of the verb *stp*] for Re." But
completely different translations are also possible, such
as "Strong with regard to the Maat of Re, whom Re
chose."

3.3. Lintel from a Temple or Palace of Ramesses II

The tile just discussed would have been part of a longer
inscription like the one more completely preserved on
this lintel. The two-line text under the winged sun disk
is very symmetrically arranged. In the middle of each
line stands the hieroglyph for "life," the ankh-sign (*ꜥnḫ*).
Left and right of this in the first line follows *nsw.t-bꜣ.t*
Wsr-mꜣꜥ.t-Rꜥ-stp-n-Rꜥ. Compare the writing of the king's
name with the writing on the faience tile. The sign
for the goddess Maat is written differently here. Both
hieroglyphs show the feather on the goddess's head,
whether she is seated on the ground or on a throne,
and it is by this feather that Maat can be recognized.
The close relationship between the words *wsr* and *mꜣꜥ.t*

in the meaning of the sentence is shown graphically by this playful writing in which Maat holds the *wsr* sign in her hand like a scepter.

In the second line is the nomen, the *z3-R^c* name of the king. The individual signs are

god with falcon head and sun disk carrying an *^cnḥ* sign	ideogram: the god Re
3 fox pelts and folded cloth	biliteral *ms* and phonetic complement *s*
folded cloth	alphabetic sign *s*, here an abbreviation for the object pronoun *sw* "him"

← 𓀭 god with two tall feathers   ideogram: the god Amun
       and the *wꜣs* scepter   (*ʾImn*)
       (= "dominion")

⊏⊐ canal   biliteral *mr*, here for the
                                      verb *mr* "love"

Together this is to be read as *Rꜥ-ms-s(w)-mr-ʾImn*, meaning "Ramesses [= Re has given him birth], beloved of Amun." Notice the way that the hieroglyph showing the god Amun is placed ahead of *mr*, although grammatically it follows it, and also that it is turned toward the name of the king he loves. The hieroglyphs *ꜥnḫ* and *wꜣs*, held by Re and Amun, are probably not to be read as part of the name; nonetheless they are not meaningless. They are attributes of the gods mentioned, which are to some extent shared with the king in whose name they appear.

At the end of each line, again symmetrically ordered on both sides, there stand the signs 𓊪𓇳𓋹𓄿 :

𓂞	*dı̓*	"give" or "given"	(see p. 18)
𓋹	*ꜥnḫ*	"life"	(see p. 34)
𓇳	*Rꜥ*	"Re"	(see p. 25)
𓏇	*mı̓*	"like"	(see p. 18)

Here the name of the god is put in front of the word *mı̓* in the now-familiar manner, although the grammatically correct ordering of the words would be *dỉ ꜥnḫ mỉ R*ꜥ "given life like Re." This formula is extremely common and is often supplemented with the word *ḏ.t* "forever"; for further examples, see pp. 59 and 61.

3.4. Fragment of a Tomb Wall

In ancient Egypt, all those who could afford to do so prepared for death during their lifetimes. Arrangements had to be made for the proper mummification and a dignified burial in a durable, well-equipped tomb, since the average Egyptian apparently regarded these things as requirements for a happy afterlife in the other world. There were, of course, skeptical voices who held that all this preparation was wasted, that the only requirement for a happy afterlife was a life lived in accordance with "Maat," the Egyptian concept of "proper conduct"; but this "proper conduct" included arranging for one's own burial, so far as it was possible.

This is the real reason that so many Egyptian objects have survived to be displayed in the museums of the world. Most of them come from tombs: statues, models, servant figures, amulets, religious books, and so forth. All these artifacts were put into the tomb with the dead person, to ensure a happy afterlife. The same purpose was served by the decoration of the tomb walls themselves with paintings and reliefs.

The fragment of tomb wall pictured, from the Egyp-

tian Museum in Berlin, shows scenes of farming in the upper register. The lower register shows the procession bringing offerings to the tomb owner, whose picture must have originally stood at the left. The hieroglyphic captions are no more than descriptions of what the people are doing. The captions describing the activities are usually infinitives (nouns that encapsulate the action of a verb, p. 36). They are best translated into English with verbs ending in "-ing." For example:

1. *wḥꜣ snṯr*
    "harvesting incense"
        For the writing of *snṯr* see p. 31.

2. *wḥꜣ ꜣšd.w*
    "harvesting *ꜣšd* fruit"
        This is probably persea fruit.

3. ʿḥb

   "filling [jars]"

4. ỉr.t ḥḏ.w

   "making [= planting] garlic"

   > For the feminine ending on the infini-
   > tive, see page 36; the biliteral *ḥḏ*
   > (p. 20) is written three times, to
   > indicate the plural (see page 37).

5. sḫp.t snṯr

   "bringing incense"

   ỉrp db.w ỉš[d.w]

   "[and] wine, figs, and *ỉšd*-fruit"

   > Notice the lovely vineyard deter-
   > minative used with *ỉrp* "wine."

The remainder of the text, which will not be explained in detail here, names still other products that
are being brought, namely "all sweet fruits and all
good fresh plants."

3.5. A Wooden Box from the Treasures of Tutankhamun

This beautiful box was made in the shape of a
cartouche. The hieroglyphs on its lid are inlaid in
ebony and tinted ivory, and give first the king's name,
Twt-ʿnḫ-ʾImn "Living image of Amun," in two bal-

anced rectangles. The group giving the name of the
god, Amun, is again put at the beginning of the name
(see p. 30). The forms of the inlays are very carefully
detailed in this example and allow us to recognize
what the biconsonantal sign *mn* ⛉ actually represents: a game board, with playing pieces set up on it.
Notice the typically Egyptian way in which this sign
combines two views of the object that could never
really be seen at the same time. The game board is
shown from the top and the pieces from the side, so
that both parts of the sign are seen from their most
characteristic angle. At the same time, the combination communicates the idea that the pieces are "on"
the board.

The third rectangle contains three hieroglyphs:

⌇	shepherd's crook	triliteral *ḥḳȝ* "ruler"
⌘	column	abbreviation for *ʾIwnw* "He-liopolis," a city near Cairo
⚘	heraldic plant of Upper Egypt (in bloom)	ideogram *šmˁ* "Upper Egypt"

ʾIwnw-šmˁ "Heliopolis of Upper Egypt" (a direct
genitive, p. 38) is another name for the city of Thebes.
So the entire inscription reads: "Tutankhamun, Ruler
of Thebes."

There are also hieroglyphs on the side of the box
that forms the base of the cartouche. In three vertical
columns stand three names of the royal titulary. The
text as a whole is framed with hieroglyphs, like the
vignette from the Book of the Dead shown on p. 77,
and forms a nicely balanced rectangle. One of the reasons for the balance is that the hieroglyphs in the first
column (from the right) look to the left, the center
column contains only hieroglyphs that are symmetri-
cal and look neither right nor left, and the hieroglyphs
in the left column all look to the right.

In the first column stands the "Horus name" of the
king, called so because as a rule there is a picture of
the falcon-god Horus above it. The actual name is written in a rectangle that may represent the enclosure wall
of the royal palace, with the niching of its facade shown
across the base. The name is to be read:

← 🐂	*k₃*	"bull"
	nḫt	"strong"
	twt	"perfect"
	ms(.wt)	"birth"

or in other words, "Strong bull, perfect [of] birth."

The second vertical line contains the *nsw.t-bi.t* name
of Tutankhamun, which was here introduced by

⊻ *nb t3.wy*   "lord of the two lands"

                                            (compare p. 37)

The name itself is to be read *Nb-ḫpr.w-R ͨ*, although it is actually written *R ͨ-ḫpr.w-nb*; see p. 30.

To the left, next to the *nsw.t-bỉ.t* name and at the same level, the *z3 R ͨ* name is written in the same form that occurs on the lid. Over this name are the words

▽ *nb ḫ ͨ.w*   "lord of Crowns"

Horizontally under the two cartouches runs the formula "Given life like Rc forever" *dỉ ͨnḫ mỉ R ͨ ḏt*; compare it with the version discussed on p. 52.

For an explanation of the god Ḥeḥ on the two knobs used to seal the box, see p. 67.

3.6. Tutankhamun's Alabaster Chest

At the time of its excavation, this small alabaster chest contained two locks of hair, each wrapped in linen. The first two lines (from the left) of the text in the rectangle that decorates its end panel should already be clear, namely,

nṯr nfr   "the good god

nb t3.wy   lord of the two lands

Nb-ḫpr.w-R ͨ   Nebkheperure"

z3 *R*^{c} "son of Re

nb ḫ^c*.w*   lord of crowns

Twt-^{c}*nḫ-*ʾ*Imn*   Tutankhamun

ḥk3 ʾ*Iwnw šm*^{c} ruler of Thebes"

Only the formula written horizontally beneath them holds something new, a second word for "forever" {⊙} , which is read *nḥḥ* (the *n* with which the word begins is not written here). The ankh-sign is written at the beginning of the formula, but it should doubtless be read as

dỉ ^{c}*nḫ ḏ.t nḥḥ*   "given life forever and ever" (see p. 52)

(The ^{c}*nḫ* sign is also written first at the end of the inscription on the top of the box and it precedes *Twt* in the name Tutankhamun. This may reflect the power of the word "life" in connection with the function of the box.)

The two words that we translate "forever" or "eternity" do not have exactly the same meaning. *Ḏt*, which has a land determinative, means infinite in space (just as we might say we could "see forever" from the top of a mountain), while *nḥḥ* with the sun determinative means infinite in time. The translation "forever and ever" thus somewhat simplifies the real meaning.

The right column of the text gives the name of the "great king's wife, Ankhesenamun," all of whose signs

have already been explained. If you have forgotten
them, you may look up *ḥm.t nsw.t* on page 32, *wr* on
p. 19, and Ankhesenamun on p. 30.

The last four hieroglyphs, written horizontally
under her cartouche, are read:

← ⸢𓂝⸣𓋹𓏏	*ꜥnḫ.tỉ*	"may she live"
𓋸𓏏	*rnp.tỉ*	"may she be young"

The hieroglyph 𓏏 is the biliteral sign *tỉ* and is
written here as a grammatical ending for the third-
person feminine singular. This ending is one of a
special group of endings attached to verbs in order
to express a wish.

The inscription on the lid of the box repeats the
king's *nsw.t-bỉ.t* name and his *zꜣ Rꜥ* name in the form
we are now well acquainted with. Before these names
stand some elaborate epithets:

𓊹𓄤	*nṯr nfr*	"the good god
𓅨	*wr*	great
𓂡𓏤𓏤𓏤𓐍𓏏	*(n)ḫt.w*	of victories" The *n* at the beginning of this word has been omitted. The striking arm here serves as a determinative.
𓉻	*ꜥꜣ*	"great

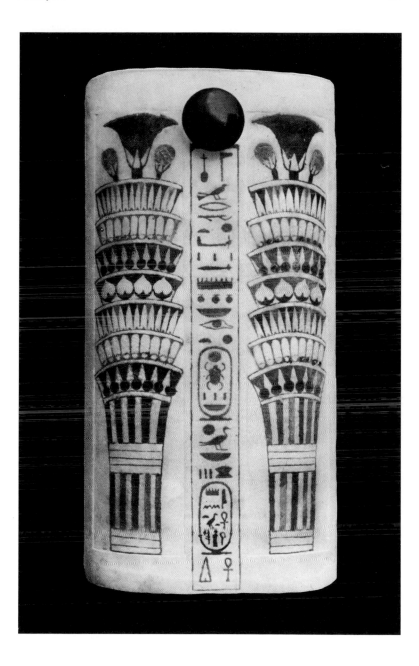

𓏶	*mn.w*	of monuments"
		This writing triples the biliteral *nw*-jar sign to indicate the plural.
𓎼	*nb*	"lord
𓁹𓏏𓎸	*ỉr.t ḫ.t*	of doing things"
		This phrase is used specifically for ritual actions.

A rather free translation of the entire inscription might then be: "The Good God, mighty of victories, great of monuments, lord of ritual, Nebkheperure, son of the sun, lord of crowns, Tutankhamun, lord of Thebes, given life."

3.7. The Alabaster Cup of Tutankhamun

The two names in cartouches have been called the *nsw.t-bỉ.t* name and the *z꜍ ꜍R* name, even when they are introduced by different titles, such as *nb t꜍.wy* or *nb ḫ*.w. The very similar rectangle of inscription on the alabaster cup shown here justifies this identification, for in the middle (first) and the left (second) line Tutankhamun's names are actually written *nsw.t-bỉ.t Nb-ḫpr.w-Rᶜ* and *z꜍ Rᶜ Twt-ᶜnḫ-ʾImn ḥk꜍ ʾIwnw-šmᶜ*.

Horizontally under these two columns is again

the formula "given life forever" (*dỉ ʿnḫ ḏ.t*). The right column (here, the third), however, contains a new text with the following signs:

← 𓇋𓏠𓈖𓊹𓏤	*ỉImn-Rʿ*	"Amun-Re
𓎟	*nb*	lord
𓊨𓊨𓊨	*ns.wt*	of thrones [p. 37]
𓏏𓄿𓈅𓈅	*tȝ.wy*	of the two lands [p. 37]
𓎟	*nb*	lord
𓊪𓏏	*p.t*	of heaven [p. 38]
𓌻𓂋𓏭𓏭	*mry*	beloved"

This line can only make sense when we realize that the name of Amun-Re and all his epithets have been placed ahead of the word *mry* out of respect for the god (see p. 30). The line is thus to be read *mry ỉImn-Rʿ nb ns.wt tȝ.wy nb p.t*, that is, "Beloved of Amun-Re, lord of the thrones of the two lands, lord of heaven."

On the rim of the cup, running to the right from the ankh-sign in the middle of the picture, the beginning of the king's titulary is visible, with the Horus name *Kȝ nḫt twt ms.wt* (see p. 58). The text running left from the ankh-sign begins:

𓋹𓂓𓎡	*ʿnḫ kȝ=k*	"May your ka live!

𓄿𓄿⳾	*ỉry=k*	May you achieve [literally, "make"]
𓁨	*ḥḥ.w*	millions
𓏤	*rnp.wt*	of years"

The biliteral sign *ḥḥ* "million" is at the same time also an ideogram for the god Ḥeḥ. This very god is shown on the handles of the cup, holding in either hand the palm branch as a sign for *rnp.t* "year."

3.8. A Canopic Coffin of Tutankhamun

In the process of mummification, the internal organs of the deceased were removed and placed in four containers, the so-called canopic jars. For the mummification of Tutankhamun, four precious miniature coffins of gold were used instead of jars. The internal organs were associated with the four "sons of Horus," each of whom had a special name: Imseti (the liver), Ḥapi (the lungs), Duamutef (the stomach), and Kebeḥsenuef (the intestines). These, in turn, were entrusted to the special protection of the four goddesses Isis, Nephthys, Neith, and Selket.

The miniature coffin shown here was for the intestines, Kebeḥsenuef. The name of this "son of Horus" is written ← 𓄖 *Ḳbḥ-sn.w=f* and means literally

"he who purifies his brother" (for the ideogram *ḳbḥ* see p. 117, W16). The intestines were under the protection of Selket (also called Serket), as the inscription explains:

← 𓂋𓏏	*ḏd mdw*	"Words to be spoken [p. 33]
𓇋𓈖	*in*	by
Zrḳ.t	*Zrḳ.t*	Selket:
dî-n=î	*dî-n=î*	I have placed [literally, given] [p. 41]
ꜥ.wy(=î)	*ꜥ.wy(=î)*	my two arms [p. 37]
ḥr	*ḥr*	upon [p. 21]
nty	*nty*	the one who
îm(=î)	*îm(=î)*	is in me [p. 42]
stp(=î)	*stp(=î)*	that I may secure [p. 116, U21]
z3	*z3*	the protection [p. 117, V17]
Ḳbḥ-sn.w=f	*Ḳbḥ-sn.w=f*	of Kebeḥsenuef
nty	*nty*	who
îm(=î)	*îm(=î)*	is in me:
Ḳbḥ-sn.w=f	*Ḳbḥ-sn.w=f*	the Kebeḥsenuef
Wsîr	*Wsîr*	of Osiris [see p. 33]

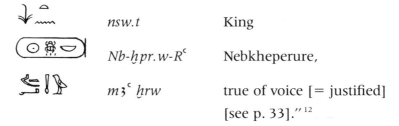

	nsw.t	King
	Nb-ḥpr.w-Rˁ	Nebkheperure,
	mꜣˁ ḫrw	true of voice [= justified] [see p. 33]."[12]

3.9. The Canopic Chest of Tutankhamun

The four canopic coffins of Tutankhamun, including
the one we have just examined, were put in a canopic
chest that was carved from a single block of alabaster.
Each coffin went into a separate compartment, which
was closed by a lid that resembled the head of the king.
At the corners of the box are the four goddesses Isis,
Nephthys, Neith, and Selket, shown in raised relief.
They stretch out their arms protectively around the
box and the internal organs of Tutankhamun within it.
Between the goddesses, on all four sides, are inscribed
short texts that state once again what is expected of
these goddesses. Each goddess has four vertical lines
of text, three facing the front or back of the sledge on
which the chest sits and one on a side panel.

The photograph shows the texts of the goddesses
Isis and Nephthys on the front of the chest. The hieroglyphs are oriented toward the middle, so that the three

12. For the reversal of the direction of writing, see p. 33.

left lines run from right to left, while the three lines on
the right run from left to right. Thus they face the same
direction as the goddess to whom they belong, which is
also true of the single lines on the side panels. The first
line of each inscription is thus the third line in from the
corner.

	ḏd mdw ỉn	"Words spoken by [p. 33]
	Nb.t-ḥw.t	Nephthys: [p. 94]
	ỉnk(=ỉ)	I clasp
	ꜥ.wy(=ỉ)	my two arms
	ḥr	around
	nty ỉm(=ỉ)	the one who is in me
	stp(=ỉ) z3	that I may secure protection
	ḥr	for
	Ḥpỉ	Ḥapi [a "son of Horus," p. 67],
	nty ỉm(=ỉ)	who is in me,
	Ḥpỉ	the Ḥapi
	Wsỉr nsw.t	of Osiris King
	Twt-ꜥnḫ-ʾImn	Tutankhamun,

𓉐𓏏𓊖𓇓	*ḥḳȝ-ʾIwnw-šmꜥ*	ruler of Thebes,
𓐙𓏏	*mȝꜥ ḫrw*	true of voice."

The three lines on the right are to be read similarly. Only three words of this text should be new to you:

← 𓊨𓊖	*ʾIs.t*	"the goddess Isis"
𓆷𓎡𓏏𓏤	*ḥȝp*	"wrap"
𓉻𓇋𓇋𓃒	*(ʾI)mztỉ*	"Imseti" (one of the sons of Horus, p. 67)

Do not be confused by the fact that some words are written differently in the right half than they are in the left. These words are:

Left Text	Right Text		
𓄿𓇋	← 𓇋𓆄	*ỉm=ỉ*	"in me"
𓁹	𓁹	*Wsỉr*	"Osiris"
𓈖𓋴	𓋴𓈖	*nsw.t*	"King"
𓐙𓏏	𓐙	*mȝꜥ ḫrw*	"true of voice"

These small graphic differences allowed the artist to make good use of the space available without making the writing look cramped. Once again you can

see how many ways there are to write hieroglyphs
"correctly."

Now you can try to read the three lines of text to
the right by yourself. If you have difficulties, the
solution is on p. 100.

3.10. Vignette from a Book of the Dead

From the New Kingdom on, the Egyptians wrote out
selected religious spells on rolls of papyrus and put
them in their tombs to ensure that they would attain a
happy life in the other world. This collection of texts is
called The Book of the Dead. Many such texts were
provided with beautiful illustrations, which can perhaps be viewed as the beginning of book illustration.

The illustration shown here is from a Book of the
Dead belonging to a man named *P₃-wi₃-n-ꜥd₃*. It is now
in the papryus collection of the National Museum of
Berlin. The picture is surrounded by a frame that is
itself made up of hieroglyphs: below is the earth sign
t₃, above is the sign for heaven *p.t*, and at the left and
right as supports of heaven are two *w₃s* scepters. The
scene itself shows the dead man, at right, pouring cool
water on the offerings that are piled upon an altar before the god Osiris. Similar illustrations are repeated in
thousands of other copies of the Book of the Dead, but
few of them are as carefully done as this one, which is

a small work of art in itself. The balance of the composition is achieved by strict divisions of the space, of which only a few examples can be briefly described here.

The rectangle is divided both vertically and, less clearly, horizontally into three parts, equal in size almost to the millimeter. The imaginary vertical lines of construction are elongations of the short register lines left of line 2 and between lines 3 and 4 of the text. The left third of the picture thus has no text at all, while the other two vertical segments contain three lines each. Almost all the diagonal lines either run parallel to the main diagonals of the rectangle (the arms of the man and the handles of the crook and flail of Osiris) or run parallel to the diagonals of the vertical segments (for example, the diagonal at the front of the pedestal bearing Osiris and his throne). The inner network of construction lines is much more finely divided than can be detailed here. Almost none of the lines of the drawing is "accidentally" placed; everything is in reality consciously planned and ordered. However, the composition also uses quite tiny deviations from the construction lines to distract the eye from the strictness of the composition and prevent an effect of forced order and stiffness.

This vignette is a good example of the indivisible connections between writing and pictures that is so characteristic of Egyptian art. The hieroglyphs that

make up the frame have already been discussed. But
some of the elements of the picture itself are also shown
in the form of certain hieroglyphs. Three of these hieroglyphs have been discussed in other sections of this
book; perhaps you can find them (the solution is on
p. 100).

But now, finally, to the text:

1. *Ḥtp-dỉ-nsw.t Wsỉr nb (n)ḥḥ*
   "An offering which the king gives to Osiris, lord of
   eternity,"
   > For the formula *ḥtp-dỉ-nsw.t* see p. 32. Behind the
   > *nb* sign is a small ⌒ , which was apparently in-
   > cluded by mistake. The word *nḥḥ* is, as is often the
   > case, written without the initial *n*; see p. 61.

2. *nṯr ꜥȝ ḫnty ỉmn.t*
   "the great god, foremost of the West,"
   > For *ḫnty* see p. 43; for *ỉmn.t* see p. 114, R14. The
   > sign ⌇ is an error for the determinative ⌇
   > (see p. 111, N25).

3. *dỉ=f ḳ(r)z(.t) nfr.t n*
   "that he may give a good burial to"

4. *ỉt-nṯr n ꞌImn-Rꜥ nsw.t nṯr.w*
   "the god's father of Amun-Re, king of the gods,"
   > For the title *ỉt-nṯr*, god's father, see p. 31.

5/6. *Pȝ-wỉȝ-n-ꜥḏȝ mȝꜥ-ḫrw*
   "Pa-wia-en-adja, true of voice."

To the left of the picture and its hieroglyphs is a text that, as you can see, is not written in hieroglyphs. This other script is called *hieratic*. It was developed from hieroglyphs by rounding and simplifying their forms and is related to them in much the same way that our handwriting is related to the printed text of a book or newspaper. In many of the hieratic signs, the hieroglyphic original can still be recognized. The beginning of the first hieratic line, for example, would look like this if it were transcribed (see p. 10) into hieroglyphs:

r3 n wn r3 n z n̄f m ḫr.t-nṭr
"A spell for opening the mouth of a man for him in the necropolis"
For *n=f* see p. 42, for *ḫr.t-nṭr* see p. 31, and for the
indirect genitive see p. 38. This is the rubric for the
so-called "opening of the mouth" ritual, which
was performed before the mummy at the funeral.

If the hieratic text is examined carefully, it is not difficult to identify the name of Pa-wia-en-adja himself. The hieratic writing of the last sign, the seated child with his hand to his mouth, hardly differs from the hieroglyphic writing in the caption of the scene at right. The direction of writing is reversed, however,

since hieratic is always written from right to left. The
name occurs twice on the hieratic page. Can you find
it? If not, please see p. 100.

3.11. The False Door of Khut-en-Ptah

Egyptian tombs were usually divided into two areas,
the closed and forbidden domain of the dead and the
more accessible area where the friends and relations of
the deceased could make prayers and offerings. The
boundary between these two areas was often marked
by a stone imitation of a door, the so-called false door.
This was decorated, as a rule, in the same manner as
the example shown here: with the name, titles, and
image of the deceased, and some short prayers.

The false door pictured is exhibited in the Egyptian
Museum of Berlin. It belongs to a woman named
Ḥw.t-n-Ptḥ (for the placement of the name
of the god Ptah at the beginning of the name, see p. 30).
Her nickname was *Ḥwȝ.t*.

The individual lines contain the following texts:

1. *Ḥtp-dỉ-nsw.t Wsỉr*
   "An offering that the king gives, and Osiris,"
   > The meaning of this formula changes over time (see
   > p. 32). In this early period the god seems to be a
   > joint donor with the king rather than a recipient of
   > the offering.

ḫnt(y) Ḏdw

"foremost of Busiris,"

> *Ḏdw* "Busiris," a town in the Delta and a principal
> cult place of the god Osiris. For the triliteral *ḫnt*, see
> pp. 24 and 43.

pr.t-ḥrw n

"a funerary offering for"

> For *prt-ḥrw* see p. 33.

im₃ḫ.t ḥr nṯr ʿ₃

"one who is venerated before the great god,"

rḫ.t nsw.t Ḥwi.t

"the king's acquaintance Khuit."

> The word *rḫ.t nsw.t* (see p. 32) is here written incor-
> rectly as *ḫr.t nsw.t.*

2/3. Lines 2 and 3 have only a single new word, the title
šps.t-nsw.t "king's noblewoman" (see p. 32). In addition, in
line 2 the epithet *ḫnty Ḏdw* is replaced by *nb Ḏdw* "lord of
Busiris."

> *prt-ḥrw n im₃ḫw.t ḥr Wsir nb* [line 3: *ḫnty*] *Ḏdw nṯr ʿ₃*
> *šps.t-nsw.t Ḥw.t-n-Ptḥ*
> "A funerary offering for the one venerated before Osiris,
> the lord [line 3: the foremost] of Busiris, the great
> god, the king's noblewoman Khut-en-Ptah."

The figure of the standing woman at the end of the lines
is naturally that of Khut-en-Ptah herself. At the same time,
however, this figure can be seen as the determinative that
belongs with a personal name—yet another example of the

close relationship between text and picture in Egyptian writing.

4. *ỉm3ḫ.t ḥr nṯr ʿ3 Ḫwỉ.t*

"One venerated before the great god, Khuit."

5. *ỉm3ḫ.t ḥr Ptḥ Zkr šps.t-nsw.t Ḫw.t-n-Ptḥ*

"One venerated before Ptah and Sokar, the king's noble-woman Khut-en-Ptah."

6. The same text as in line 5, although in a slightly different order. In reversing the direction of the individual hieroglyphs, the stonecarver accidentally carved one sign exactly as it is in line 5 rather than its mirror image. Can you find which sign was not correctly turned? (The solution is on p. 101.)

7. *ỉm3ḫ.t Ḫw.t-n-Ptḥ*

8. *šps.t-nsw.t ỉm3ḫ.t Ḫwỉ.t*

9/10. *ỉm3ḫ.t ḥr nṯr ʿ3 Ḫwỉ.t*

Now only the few hieroglyphs in the rectanglar "window" above the door remain to be discussed. Directly over the picture of the deceased you will recognize the name *Ḫwỉ.t*, written vertically, and above that the preposition *n*, "for Khuit." To the right of these the biliteral ⚱ *ḥ3* is repeated six times, each representing the number "1,000." Under each of these signs is carved an abbreviation for one of the commodities that

the deceased needs by the thousand for life in the other world: bread (⊖), beer (ᴂ), alabaster (jars with oil) (४), and clothing (ᵛᵛᵛ),[13] all (ᴗ) cattle (⋈) and birds (⼢). This is a very short version of an extremely common formula that occurs on funerary monuments of all periods of Egyptian history. We will encounter it again in the next example, which was made about fifteen hundred years after the false door of Khut-en-Ptah.

3.12. The Tomb Stela of Tashep-Khonsu

In the Egyptian Late Period, members of the growing middle class honored their deceased relatives with small tomb steles, which were relatively cheap in both materials (usually wood) and workmanship. Many hundreds of examples are collected in the museums of the world, often carelessly or even sloppily made, testimony to a method of mass production lacking any artistic pride.

The stela of Tashep-Khonsu (whose name is also written more fully Tashep-en-Khonsu) belongs among the better examples of this type because of the relatively

---

13. This is a variant form of the sign; more normally the hieroglyph S27 (see p. 114) occurs in this position.

careful painting of its text and pictures. The stela is exhibited in the Egyptian Museum in Berlin.

The scene shows, at right, the deceased woman in prayer before five divinities. The two columns of hieroglyphs above her, like the woman herself, are oriented toward the gods, so that they can read them:

Wsỉr nb.t pr Tȝ-šp-Ḫnsw mȝꜥ-ḫrw

"Osiris Mistress of a House Tashep-Khonsu, true of voice."

The letter *n* is here, as in the rest of the stela, written not as ∿∿∿ but as ⎯ . Above and slightly to the right of the divinities are written their names. They are turned so as to be read from the viewpoint of Tashep-Khonsu and include the following:

Rꜥ		"Re" The sun determinative here is decorated with a cobra, like the one on the god's head.
ꜣIs.t nb(.t) pt		"Isis, mistress of heaven"
Nb.t-ḥw.t nb(.t) pt		"Nephthys, mistress of heaven"

The names of the other two gods are almost entirely destroyed. The five horizontal lines below this scene are to be read as follows:

Ḥtp-dỉ nsw.t Rˤ-Ḥr-ȝḫ.ty

"An offering which the king gives to Re-Harakhti,"

   For the name of the god Re-Harakhti, see p. 94.

ḥr(y) nṯr.w

"the highest of the gods,"

   Ḥr(y) "highest" (see p. 43) is here written with the

   sky-sign as a determinative.

Tm nb ȝ.wy (nb) ᵓIwnw

"and to Atum, lord of the two lands, [lord of] Heliopolis"

   The second sign of the word *Tm* is the biliteral sign *tm*,

   which is augmented here with the phonetic comple-

   ments *t* and *m*. The actual writing is thus *t-tm-m*;

   compare page 22.

nṯr ˤȝ nb tp (an error for *p.t*)

"the great god, lord of heaven"

dỉ=f ḫȝ m tȝ ḫȝ m ḥḳt

"that he may give 1,000 of bread, 1,000 of beer . . ."

   Here begins the formula that was written in abbreviated form on the false door in the previous example
(p. 83). The preposition *m* here means "portions of."
The number actually refers to the appropriate unit,
so that what is really meant is something like "1,000
loaves of bread, 1,000 jars of beer," and so forth.

ḫȝ m ỉḥ.w ḫȝ m ȝpd.w

"1,000 of cattle, 1,000 of birds,"

ḫȝ m snṯr ḫȝ m ḳbḥ

"1,000 of incense, 1,000 of libations,"

For the writing of *snṯr* see p. 31.

ḫȝ m ḫ.t nb.t nfr(.t)

"1,000 of every good thing"

n kȝ n Wsỉr nb(.t) pr

"for the soul of the Osiris, the mistress of a house,"

The dead woman is equated with the male god Osiris; see p. 33.

Tȝ-šp-n-Ḫnsw mȝꜥ ḫrw

"Tashep-en-Khonsu, true of voice,"

An *n* has been inserted into the name here, a variant that was mentioned above. The small *t* at the end of the name before the seated-woman determinative is here simply a graphic indication of the feminine, and should not be read.

ms nb(.t) pr Dỉ-Bȝst(.t)-p(ȝ)-snb mȝꜥ ḫrw ỉmȝḫw(.t)

"born to the mistress of a house Di-Bastet-pa-seneb, true of voice, a venerated one."

3.13. The Hieroglyphs on the Cover: A Temple Inscription

The hieroglyphic text on the cover of this book is taken from the "White Chapel" of King Senwosret I (1971–1929 B.C.), now reconstructed at the open-air museum

in the Karnak temple complex. The colors of the hieroglyphs were not preserved in the original, but they
have been restored here from other inscriptions. The
inscription is a variant on a very common form. It is to
be read as follows:

ḏd mdw in 'Imn-Rᶜ nb ns.wt t3.wy
"Words spoken by Amun-Re, lord of the thrones of the
Two Lands:"

> For *ḏd mdw*, see p. 33; for *ns.wt*, see p. 37; and for
> *t3.wy*, see p. 37.

di̯-n(=i̯) ᶜnḫ ḏd w3s nb n z3(=i̯) Ḫpr-k3-Rᶜ
"I have given all life, all stability, and all dominion to my
son Kheperkare;"

> For the omission of the suffix pronoun =i̯, see p. 40; for
> the verb form *sḏm-n=f*, see p. 41.

di̯-n(=i̯) n=f ḥw nb ḫr=i̯
"I have given to him all sustenance with me."

Although in this text the god is speaking about the
king, the divinity more often speaks to the king directly: *di̯-n(=i̯) n=k . . .* , "I have given to you. . . ."
This speech appears very frequently in texts accom-
panying temple offering scenes of all periods. In addition to the most common benefits (life, stability, and
dominion) that are mentioned here, the king frequently
receives *snb* ("health"), *3w.t ib* ("happiness"), and *ḥḥw
rnp.wt* ("millions of years"). See pp. 38 and 67. Such

speeches usually accompany a scene in which the king is making an offering or performing a ritual service for the divinity. Such scenes were later copied and adapted by nonroyal people in their funerary texts, as in the text on p. 77.

4. CONCLUSION

4.1. Selected Royal Names

Some of the most important rulers' names are listed
below, in their historical order. The main spelling given
is the normal spelling of the Egyptian form. Greek
forms, which are often used in older books, are given in
parentheses. The numbers under the "Usual Spelling"
column refer to the sign list (Section 5.3).

Writing	Transliteration	Usual Spelling
	$Mn\breve{\imath}$	Menes Y5-N35-M17
	$Snfrw$	Snefru S29 F35-I9-D21-G43
	$Ḥwfw$	Khufu (Cheops) Aa1-G43-I9-G43
	$Ḥ^c=f\text{-}R^c$	Khafre (Chephren) N5-N28-I9
	$Mn\text{-}k\ni w\text{-}R^c$	Menkaure (Mycerinus) N5-Y5-D28-D28-D28
	$S\ni ḥw\text{-}R^c$	Sahure N5-D61-G43

Writing	Transliteration	Usual Spelling
	Mnṯw-ḥtp	Mentuhotep Y5-N35-V13-G43-R4- X1-Q3
	ʾImn-m-ḥȝ.t	Amenemhat M17-Y5-N35-G17-F4-X1
	Z-n-wsrt	Senwosret (Sesostris) F12-S29-D21-X1-O34- N35
	ʾImn-ḥtp	Amenhotep (Amenophis) M17-Y5-N35-R4-X1-Q3
	Ḏḥwty-ms	Thutmose (Tuthmosis) G26-F31-S29
	Ḥȝ.t-šps.wt	Hatshepsut F4-X1-Z1-A51-X1-Z2
	ȝḫ-n-ʾItn	Akhenaton M17-X1-N35-N5-G25- Aa1-N35
	Twt-ꜥnḫ-ʾImn	Tutankhamun M17-Y5-N35-X1-G43-X1- S34
	Rꜥ-ms-s	Ramses (Ramesses) N5-F31-S29-S29

Writing	Transliteration	Usual Spelling
(image of cartouche)	*T₃hrwḳ*	Taharka N17-O4-E23-N29
(image of cartouche)	*Psmṯk*	Psamtik (Psammeticus) Q3-S29-G17-V13-V31
(image of cartouche)	*T₃rywš₃*	Darius N16-D21-M17-M17- Z7-M8
(image of cartouche)	*Ptrwmys*	Ptolemy Q3-X1-E23-Z7-Aa13- M17-M17-S29
(image of cartouche)	*Kysrz*	Caesar (Augustus, etc.) V31-M17-M17-S29-D21- O34

4.2. Names of Gods

Only the names of gods given in this book are listed.

Writing	Variants	Transliteration	Usual Spelling
(image)	(image)	*ʾImn*	Amun
(image)	(image) and ⊙	*Rᶜ*	Re
(image)		*ʾImn-Rᶜ*	Amun-Re

Writing	Variants	Transliteration	Usual Spelling
		ʾItn	Aton
		Ḥr	Horus
		Ḥr-ȝḫ.ty	Harakhti (= Horus of the Horizon)
		Rˁ-Ḥr-ȝḫ.ty	Re-Harakhti
		Ḥw.t-Ḥr	Hathor (= Mansion of Horus)
		ʾIs.t	Isis
	and	Wsỉr	Osiris
		Ptḥ	Ptah
		Zkr	Sokar
		Ḫnsw	Khonsu
		Ḏḥwty	Thoth
		(ʾI)tm	Atum
		Ḥḥ	Heh
		Zrḳ.t	Selket
		Nb.t-ḥw.t	Nephthys (= Mistress of the Mansion)

Writing	Variants	Transliteration	Usual Spelling
		B3st(.t)	Bastet
		M3ᶜ.t	Maat
		(ˀI)mzty	Imseti
		Ḥpy	Hapi
		Ḳbḥ-sn.w=f	Kebehsenuef

4.3. Further Study of Hieroglyphs

If you have read this far, the system of Egyptian hieroglyphic writing has, I hope, become somewhat more
comprehensible to you. You can now read and translate many short inscriptions by yourself, such as those
inscribed on the precious objects in the treasure of
Tutankhamun. More than that is beyond the scope of
this book.

But perhaps your curiosity has just been awakened.
In that case, there are a number of ways you can learn
still more about the writing and language of the ancient
Egyptians. The next step may be the second volume of
Hieroglyphs without Mystery, which is planned for the
future. It will include further examples of hieroglyphic
texts, explained in the same manner, and among them
longer inscriptions from famous Egyptian monuments.

Other chapters will give overviews of the art and scope
of Egyptian literature, Egyptian and non-Egyptian
writing systems derived from hieroglyphs, and the
story of the decipherment of the script.

You can also, of course, continue to work independently using one of the available grammars of Egyptian
(see the list on p. 102). It should be noted, however,
that none of these grammars are especially well suited
to self-instruction. It is in any case much easier to continue your study of Egyptian writing and language under the direction of a teacher. Many universities with
departments of Egyptology, Near Eastern languages, or
ancient art and archaeology occasionally offer courses
in Egyptian hieroglyphs through their extension divisions, as do some museums with large collections of
Egyptian art.

Universities in the United States and Canada that
currently have active programs in Egyptology are
Brown University, the University of California at Ber-
keley and at Los Angeles, the University of Chicago, the
Johns Hopkins University, Memphis State University,
New York University, the University of Pennsylvania,
the University of Toronto, and Yale University. You
might also be able to find information about courses in
your area through the American Research Center in
Egypt, which has its American headquarters at New
York University, or the Society for the Study of Ancient
Egypt, headquartered at the University of Toronto.

In Great Britain, there are programs in Egyptology

at the universities of Birmingham, Cambridge, Edinburgh, Liverpool, Manchester, and Oxford, and at University College in London. The Egypt Exploration Society in London may also be able to suggest an appropriate course. Egyptology is taught at Macquarie University in Australia and at the University of Auckland in New Zealand. Speakers of English living in Cairo may be able to arrange courses through the American University in Cairo.

If there is no adult education course available in your area, it is often possible to arrange a correspondence course through one of these university departments, perhaps with an advanced graduate student. If you live near one of the universities mentioned, you might also ask about the possibility of auditing one of their courses in the ancient Egyptian language. Such courses are designed primarily for the training of professional Egyptologists, however, and may require more work than is practical for those with other responsibilities. Another option is to find out whether your local community college could offer a course. If there is sufficient interest in hieroglyphs, an instructor can often be found by inquiring at one of the institutions listed above or at your local art museum.

Whichever method you select, I wish you much enjoyment and success in your further study of ancient Egyptian hieroglyphs, one of the oldest writing systems in human history, and one that becomes more fascinating the further its mysteries are penetrated.

5. APPENDIXES

5.1. Solutions to the Problems

Page 14
The names in the left column are Robert, Charles, William, Gregory, Martin, and Alexander. The names in the right column are Mary, Elizabeth, Susan, Patricia, Sharon, and Cleopatra.

Page 23
The royal names shown in cartouches are:

Mnỉ = Menes
Ḫwfw = Khufu (= Cheops)
Tȝhrwḳ = Taharka
Psmṯk = Psamtik (= Psammeticus)
Tȝrỉwšȝ = Darius
Ptrwmỉz = Ptolemy

(Greek forms of the names that are used in some history books are given in parentheses.) See also p. 91 for a fuller list of kings.

Page 28
𓀾   a mummy; used as a determinative for words like mummy, statue, picture, or image

　　　　　　a seated woman

　　　　　　a staff wrapped in cloth, which flaps loose at the
　　　　　　　　top; used as a determinative for the names of
　　　　　　　　gods

　　　　　　the canopy of heaven, with supports at the
　　　　　　　　corners

　　　　　　a tied and sealed papyrus roll, which serves as a
　　　　　　　　determinative for anything related to writing,
　　　　　　　　as well as abstract ideas

　　　　　　a grapevine; used in words connected with
　　　　　　　　grapes or wine

　　　　　　the flat land sign, which occurs in the word *ḏt*
　　　　　　　　"eternity, forever" as well as in words related
　　　　　　　　to land or agriculture

Page 31

The first writing of the word *snṯr* "incense" shows that
the *nṯr*-sign is placed first, in honor of its divine nature.
The real initial consonant, *s*, follows. Finally come the
phonetic complements *ṯ* and *r* and three small circles,
which here do not stand for the plural, but instead for
the many tiny pellets that make up a quantity of incense. The second writing also begins with the *nṯr*-sign.
It uses the biliteral sign *sn* and the alphabetic signs *ṯ* and
r, followed by the same three small circles.

Page 74

ḏd mdw n ʾIs.t	Words spoken by Isis:
ḥȝp(=ỉ) ʿ.wy(=ỉ)	I wrap my arms
ḥr nty ỉm(=ỉ)	around the one who is in me
stp(=ỉ) zȝ ḥr	that I may secure protection for
Mzty nty ỉm(=ỉ)	Imsety who is in me,
Mzty Wsỉr	the Imsety of Osiris
nsw.t	King
Nb-ḥpr.w-Rʿ	Nebkheperure,
mȝʿ-ḥrw	true of voice.

Page 78

The hieroglyphs "hidden" in the vignette that have already been introduced in this book are as follows:

the scepter of Osiris (*ḥḳȝ*)
the jar pouring in the hand of the deceased a libation (*ḳbḥ*)
the pedestal on which the throne of Osiris rests (*mȝʿ*)

Other elements of the vignette that are identical to common hieroglyphs include the flail in the hand of Osiris, his throne, and the offering table.

Page 81

The hieratic writing of the name *Pȝ-wỉȝ-n-ʿḏȝ* looks like this:

It can be found at the end of the first line (with the determinative at the beginning of the second line) and also at the beginning of the ninth line (with the first sign at the end of the eighth line). If these hieratic signs are transcribed into hieroglyphs, the name appears as

If you compare this with the original hieroglyphic writing of the same name in the vignette, you will immediately notice a number of differences. These differences will not be discussed here, except to note that they once again demonstrate the variety of "correct" writings.

Page 83
The sign that should have been reversed in line 6, but by mistake was made in the same direction as in line 5, is the basket with a handle. This sign serves as the alphabetic sign *k* in the name of the god Sokar, *Zkr*.

5.2. Books on Egyptian Vocabulary and Grammar

The following grammars are used most often for introductory courses in ancient Egyptian. They are best studied in consultation with a teacher. Grammars by

Sir E. A. Wallis Budge and Samuel Mercer, although
widely available, are many years out of date and are
likely to confuse the beginner.

Brunner, Helmut. *An Outline of Middle Egyptian
    Grammar*. Trans. by B. Ockinga. Graz (Austria):
    Akademische Druck- und Verlagsanstalt, 1979.
Gardiner, Sir Alan. *Egyptian Grammar, Being an Introduc-
    tion to the Study of Hieroglyphs*. 3d ed. rev. London:
    Oxford University Press, 1957.

Professional Egyptologists are fortunate in having the
monumental seven-volume *Wörterbuch der ägyptischen
Sprachen* to consult in their research. For students, however, a less exhaustive dictionary is more convenient.

Faulkner, R. O. *A Concise Dictionary of Middle Egyptian*.
    Oxford: Griffith Institute, 1962.

For help in drawing hieroglyphic signs and for inter-
esting notes about their variation, see:

Fischer, H. G. *Ancient Egyptian Calligraphy: A Beginner's
    Guide to Writing Hieroglyphs*. 2d ed. New York:
    Metropolitan Museum of Art, 1983.

For further examples and discussions (technical, but
fascinating) of the orientation of hieroglyphs and their
relationships with the scenes, objects, and buildings
they decorate, see:

Fischer, H. G. *The Orientation of Hieroglyphs. Part I: Reversals.* Egyptian Studies No 2. New York: Metropolitan Museum of Art, 1977.

5.3. Hieroglyphic Sign List

In the following list, all the hieroglyphs introduced in this book are collected and their use explained. Alphabetic signs are more fully explained on pages 11–13, and most of the biliterals are listed on pages 18–20. As a convenience for those who wish to go on with their studies, the order used is the same as that used in the Sign List section of Gardiner's *Egyptian Grammar*, which is used by almost all modern Egyptologists. At the same time, the numbers will give you an idea how small the selection of hieroglyphs used here is, compared to the number in use during the Middle Kingdom. It should also be noted that the meanings and usages of signs given here are by no means complete.

A. *Men and their Activities*

1	𓀀	Seated man
		det. (p. 14); suffix pronoun I, me (p. 39)
9	𓀞	Man carrying a basket
		det. (p. 21)
17	𓀔	Seated child
		det. (p. 78)

19		Bent man, leaning on a stick
		det. (p. 27)
24		Man striking with a stick
		det. (p. 27)
29		Man standing on his head
		det. (p. 27)
40		Seated god with beard and long wig
		det. (p. 72); suffix pronoun I, me (p. 39)
51		Man seated on a chair holding a flail
		ideogram *šps* "noble" (p. 32)
53		Mummy
		det. (p. 16)
54		Reclining mummy
		det. (p. 78)

B. *Women and their Activities*

1		Seated woman
		det. (p. 14); suffix pronoun I, me (p. 39)

C. *Gods and Goddesses in Human Form*

2		God with falcon head and sun disk
		ideogram *Rᶜ* "Re" (p. 51)
10		Goddess with feather on her head
		ideogram *M3ᶜ.t* "Maat" (p. 49)
—		Goddess on throne with feather on her head
		variant of C10 (p. 51)

11	𓁨	God with raised hands and the year sign (M4) on his head *Ḥḥ* "[the god] Ḥeḥ"; biliteral *ḥḥ* "million" (p. 67)
12	𓁩	God with two tall plumes on his head ideogram *ʾImn* "Amun" (p. 52)

D. Parts of the Human Body

2	𓁶	Face biliteral *ḥr* (p. 19); preposition *ḥr* "upon" (p. 21)
3	𓄹	Hair det. (p. 29)
4	𓁹	Eye biliteral *ỉr* (p. 19); verb *ỉr* "to do, to make" (p. 21)
19	𓄞	Nose triliteral *ḫnt* (p. 24)
21	𓂋	Mouth alphabetic sign *r* (p. 11); ideogram *rꜣ* "mouth, speech" (p. 5)
28	𓂓	Raised arms biliteral *kꜣ* (p. 18), *kꜣ* "kа" (p. 21)
32	𓂩	Embracing arms det. (p. 72)
36	𓂝	Arm alphabetic sign ꜥ (p. 11)

37	⌒	Arm and hand with sign X8
		biliteral *dỉ* (p. 18); verb *dỉ* "to give"
		(p. 40)
40	⌒	Arm and hand with a stick
		ideogram *nḫt* "strong" (p. 58); det.
		(p. 62)
46	⌒	Hand
		alphabetic sign *d* (p. 12)
54	⌒	Walking legs
		det. (p. 27)
55	⌒	Backward walking legs
		det. (p. 27)
58	⌊	Leg
		alphabetic sign *b* (p. 11)
61	ⱶⱶⱶ	Toes
		triliteral *sꜣḥ* (p. 24)

E. Mammals

1	🐂	Bull
		det. (p. 21)
2	🐂	Attacking bull
		ideogram *kꜣ* "bull" (p. 58)
23	🦁	Lion
		biliteral *rw* (p. 19); used for *l* in foreign
		words
34	🐇	Hare
		biliteral *wn* (p. 28)

F. *Parts of Mammals*

1		Head of an ox
		abbreviation for *ỉḥ(.w)* "cattle"
		(pp. 85, 87)
4		Front part of a lion
		ideogram *ḥȝ.t* "front, foremost"
12		Head and neck of a jackal or a similar animal
		triliteral *wsr* (p. 49)
31		Three joined fox pelts
		biliteral *ms* (p. 20)
32		Animal belly with teats
		alphabetic sign *ḫ* (p. 12)
34		Heart
		ideogram *ỉb* "heart" (p. 25)
35		Heart and windpipe
		triliteral *nfr* (p. 23)
39		Ribs with marrow escaping on one side
		ideogram *ỉmȝḫ* "venerated" (p. 33)
40		Ribs with marrow escaping on both sides
		biliteral *ȝw* (p. 38)

G. *Birds*

1		Egyptian vulture
		alphabetic sign *ȝ* (p. 11)
5		Falcon
		ideogram *Ḥr* "[god] Horus" (p. 94)

17	Owl
	alphabetic sign *m* (p. 11)
25	Ibis
	biliteral ꜣḫ (p. 92)
26	Ibis on a standard
	ideogram *Ḏḥwty* "[god] Thoth" (p. 94)
36	Swallow
	biliteral *wr* (p. 21)
37	Sparrow
	det. for bad or small things (p. 29)
39	Duck
	biliteral *zꜣ* (p. 18); *zꜣ* "son" (p. 21)
40	Duck in flight
	biliteral *pꜣ* (p. 18)
41	Duck in flight
	graphic variant of G40
43	Quail chick
	alphabetic sign *w* (p. 11)

H. Parts of Birds

1	Head of a duck
	abbreviation for ꜣ*pd.w* "birds"
	(pp. 85, 87)
8	Egg
	det. in names of goddesses (p. 86)

I. Amphibians and Reptiles

9   Horned viper

alphabetic sign *f* (p. 11); not read in the
word *ỉt* "father" (p. 26)

10   Cobra

alphabetic sign *ḏ* (p. 12); in *ḏd mdw*
"words spoken" (or similar constructions,
p. 33)

K. Fish

1   Fish (*tilapia nilotica*)

biliteral *ỉn* (pp. 19, 72)

L. Insects

1   Beetle

triliteral *ḫpr* (p. 23)

2   Bee

ideogram *bỉ.t* "bee" (p. 25); in *nsw.t-bỉ.t*
"king of Upper and Lower Egypt" (p. 47)

M. Trees and Plants

1   Tree

det. (p. 36)

3   Branch

biliteral *ḫt* (p. 62)

4	}	Palm branch without leaves
		triliteral *rnp*; in *rnp.t* "year" (p. 67)
7	}	Combination of M4 and Q3
		ideogram *rnp* "to be young" (p. 62)
8	⊔⊔⊔	Pool with lotus blossoms
		biliteral *š3* (p. 18)
12	⚘	Lotus plant
		biliteral *ḥ3* (p. 18); *ḥ3* "1,000" (pp. 83, 87)
16	⚘	Clump of papyrus plants
		biliteral *ḥ3* (p. 18)
17	⚘	Reed leaf
		alphabetic sign *i̭* (p. 11)
23	⚘	Heraldic plant of Upper Egypt (sedge?)
		biliteral *sw* (p. 19); in *nsw.t* "king of Upper Egypt" (p. 32)
26	⚘	Blossoming plant (M23)
		ideogram *šmꜥ* "Upper Egypt" (p. 57)
43	⚘	Grape arbor
		det. (p. 21)

N. Sky, Earth, Water

1	▭	Sky
		ideogram *p.t* "sky"; det. (p. 86)
5	⊙	Sun
		ideogram *rꜥ* "sun" (p. 25); det. for sun and words concerning time (p. 61)

6	𓇴	Sun with uraeus
		ideogram *Rꜥ* "Re" (p. 86)
8	𓇶	Sun with rays
		det. (p. 29)
14	𓇼	Star
		ideogram *sbꜣ* "star" (p. 25)
16	𓇾	Land with grains of sand
		ideogram *tꜣ* "earth, land"; det. in
		"forever" (p. 46)
17	𓇿	Land
		variant of M16
19	𓈃	Two sandy plains
		ideogram *ꜣḫ.ty* in the name of the god
		Harakhti (p. 94)
21	𓈅	Tongue of land
		det. for land (p. 66)
25	𓈉	Hilly land
		det. for places and people outside the Nile
		Valley and Egypt (p. 78)
28	𓈍	Hill with the rising sun
		biliteral *ḫꜥ* (p. 18); "crown" (p. 59)
29	𓈎	Sandy hillside
		alphabetic sign *ḳ* (p. 12)
33	𓈒	Three grains of sand
		det. for the plural of certain words
35	𓈖	Line of water
also	—	alphabetic sign *n* (p. 11)

		Three lines of water det. for liquids (p. 55)
36		Canal biliteral *mr* (p. 19); *mr* "love" (p. 52)
37		Lake alphabetic sign *š* (p. 12)
42		Well with water biliteral *ḥm* (p. 26)

O. Buildings and Parts of Buildings

1		Plan of a house ideogram *pr* "house" (p. 21); biliteral *pr* (p. 19)
3		Combination of signs O1, P8, X3, and W22 Abbreviation for *pr.t-ḫrw* "offering" (p. 33)
4		Courtyard alphabetic sign *h* (p. 11)
6		Rectangular enclosure in plan ideogram *ḥw.t* "mansion, temple"
9		Combination of signs O6, V30, and X1 writing of *Nb.t-ḥw.t* "[the goddess] Nephthys" (p. 86)
10		Combination of signs O6 and G5 writing of *Ḥwt-Ḥr* "[the goddess] Hathor" (p. 94)

28	Pillar
	triliteral *iwn*; abbreviation for *'Iwnw* "Heliopolis" (p. 57)
29	Column
	biliteral *ꜥꜣ* (p. 18); *ꜥꜣ* "great" (p. 21)
31	Door panel (turned on its side)
	det. for "open" (p. 28)
34	Door bolt
	alphabetic sign *z* (p. 12)
49	Town with crossroads
	det. (p. 29)

P. Ships and Parts of Ships

3	Sacred barque
	ideogram *wiꜣ* "divine barque" (p. 78)
8	Rudder (steering oar)
	triliteral *ḥrw* (p. 24); in *mꜣꜥ-ḥrw* "true of voice," or "justified" (p. 33)

Q. Furniture

1	Seat
	ideogram *s.t* "place"; biliteral *is* in *'Is.t* "[the goddess] Isis" (p. 73), biliteral *ws* in *Wsir* "[the god] Osiris" (p. 73)
2	Carrying chair
	biliteral *ws* in *Wsir* "[the god] Osiris" (p. 73)

| 3 | ▢ | Stool |
| | | alphabetic sign *p* (p. 11) |

R. Temple Equipment

4	⊖	Bread offering on a mat
		triliteral *ḥtp* (p. 24)
7	⌘	Cup with burning incense
		abbreviation in the title *it-nṯr* (p. 31)
8	⌐	Staff wrapped with a strip of cloth
		ideogram *nṯr* "god" (p. 25); det. in names
		of divinities (p. 86)
11	▯	Pillar
		biliteral *ḏd*; abbreviation for *ḏd* "stability"
		(p. 46); in the name of the city *Ḏdw*
		"Busiris" (p. 82)
14	⸙	Standard with a feather
		ideogram *imn.t* "western" (p. 78)

S. Crowns, Clothing, and Staves

3	⩘	Red crown of Lower Egypt
		alphabetic sign *n* (p. 13)
27	⊥⊥	Edge of cloth with a fringe
		abbreviation for *mnḫ.t* "clothing"
—	▵▵▵	Variant of S27 (p. 85)
28	▨	Cloth with fringe and sign S29
		det. for clothing and cloth (p. 73)

29   Folded cloth
        alphabetic sign *s* (p. 12); abbreviation
        for *snb* "health" (p. 34)

34   Looped knot
        triliteral *ꜥnḫ*; in *ꜥnḫ* "life" (p. 34)

38   Shepherd's crook
        triliteral *ḥḳꜣ*; in *ḥḳꜣ* "ruler" (p. 57)

40   Scepter with the head of an animal
        triliteral *wꜣs*; abbreviation for *wꜣs*
        "dominion" (p. 30)

43   Walking stick
        triliteral *mdw*; in *ḏd-mdw* "words spoken"
        or "recitation" (p. 33)

T. Equipment for War, Hunting, and Butchery

3   Mace
        biliteral *ḥḏ* (p. 55)

22   Arrowhead
        biliteral *sn* (p. 40)

23   Graphic variant of S22 (p. 67)

28   Chopping block
        biliteral *ḫr* (p. 31)

U. Agriculture and Crafts

1   Sickle
        biliteral *mꜣ* (p. 18)

4   Combination of U1 and Aa11
abbreviation for *mꜣꜥ* "true" (p. 33)

6   Hoe
biliteral *mr* (p. 19); *mr* "love" (p. 21)

13   Plow
det. (p. 27)

15   Sledge
biliteral *tm* (p. 79); in the name of the god
Atum (p. 87)

21   Adze
triliteral *stp* (p. 24); in *stp* "choose"
(p. 49); *stp zꜣ* "secure protection" (p. 69)

28   Drill for starting fire
biliteral *ḏꜣ* (p. 18); abbreviation for *wḏꜣ*
"prosperity" (p. 34)

33   Pestle
biliteral *tỉ* (p. 62)

V. Rope and Baskets

4   Lasso
biliteral *wꜣ* (p. 18)

6   Rope
abbreviation for alabaster (jar) (p. 85)

10   "Cartouche"
det. surrounding royal name (p. 29)

13   Hobble
alphabetic sign *ṯ* (p. 12)

17		Rolled herdsman's mat, tied in a loop
		ideogram *z3* "protection" (p. 69)
28		Wick of twisted flax
		alphabetic sign *ḥ* (p. 12)
30		Woven basket
		biliteral *nb* (p. 19); *nb* "every, all" (p. 21);
		nb "lord" (p. 38)
31		Basket with handle
		alphabetic sign *k* (p. 12)

W. Vessels

2		Sealed jar of salve
		triliteral *b3s*; in the name of the goddess
		Bastet (p. 88)
11		Jar stand
		ideogram *ns.t* "throne" (p. 37); alphabetic
		sign *g* (p. 12)
15		Tall water jar
		ideogram *ḳbḥ* "purify," "poured offering"
		(p. 100)
16		Tall water jar in a jar stand
		graphic variant of W15 (p. 69)
17		Three water jars in stands
		triliteral *ḫnt* (p. 24); *ḫnt(y)* "first, fore-
		most" (pp. 43, 82)
18		Four water jars in stands
		graphic variant of W17

19   ⚱   Milk jug in a sling
            biliteral *mỉ* (p. 53)

22   ⊎   Beer jug
            ideogram *ḥnḳ.t* "beer" (p. 85); det. (p. 87)

24   ʊ   Spherical jar
            biliteral *nw* (p. 18)

X. Bread and Cakes

1   ⌂   Bread
            alphabetic sign *t* (p. 12)

2   θ   Bread
            ideogram *t3* "bread"

3   0   Bread
            graphic variant of X3

4   ⬭   Bread
            det. for *pr.t-ḫrw* (p. 82); sign similar
            to N17

8   △   Conical bread?
            biliteral *dỉ* (p. 18); verb *dỉ* "give" (p. 40)

Y. Writing, Games, and Music

1   ⟋⟍   Sealed papyrus roll (also vertical)
            det. for writing, abstract ideas

5   ⛶   Game board
            biliteral *mn* (p. 19)

Z. *Strokes and Abbreviated Signs*

1	ı	Stroke
		det. for "1"; det. stroke (p. 5)
2	ııı	Three strokes
		det. for plural (p. 37)
3		Three strokes
		graphic variant of Z2
4	ıı	Two small strokes
also	//	det. for dual (p. 37); alphabetic sign *y* (p. 13)
7	ꝑ	Hieroglyph formed from the hieratic writing of the sign G43
		alphabetic sign *w* (p. 13)

Aa. *Signs of Doubtful Origin*

1	⊜	Placenta?
		alphabetic sign *ẖ* (p. 12)
5		Part of a steering oar?
		biliteral *ḥp* (p. 19); in the name of the god Hapi (p. 72)
11		Platform? (also vertical)
		triliteral *mꜣꜥ*; in *mꜣꜥ-ḫrw* "true of voice, justified (p. 33)
13		?
		alphabetic sign *m* (p. 13)

5.4 Museum Numbers and Photo Credits
for the Objects Discussed

1. Architrave: Egyptian Museum, Berlin. Accession number 340/67.

2. Tile: State Collection of Egyptian Art, Munich. Accession number ÄS 5535.

3. Lintel: Egyptian Museum, Berlin. Accession number 8/66.

4. Tomb wall: Egyptian Museum, Berlin. Accession number 3/65.

5. Wooden box: Egyptian Museum, Cairo. JE 61490. "Treasures of Tutankhamun Exhibition," 1976–1979, catalog number 28. European Tutankhamun Exhibition, 1980–1981, catalog number 6.

6. Alabaster box (two views): Egyptian Museum, Cairo. JE 61762. "Treasures of Tutankhamun Exhibition," 1976–1979, catalog number 9. European Tutankhamun Exhibition, 1980–1981, catalog number 46.

7. Alabaster cup: Egyptian Museum, Cairo. JE 62125. "Treasures of Tutankhamun Exhibition," 1976–1979, catalog number 2. European Tutankhamun Exhibition, 1980–1981, catalog number 39.

8. Canopic coffin: Egyptian Museum, Cairo. JE 60691. "Treasures of Tutankhamun Exhibition," 1976–1979, catalog number 45. European Tutankhamun Exhibition, 1980–1981, catalog number 45.

9. Canopic box: Egyptian Museum, Cairo. JE 60687. "Treasures of Tutankhamun Exhibition," 1976–1979, catalog number 44 (stopper only). European Tutankhamun Exhibition, 1980–1981, catalog number 38.

10. Book of the Dead: Papyrus collection of the National Museum in Berlin. Accession number P 10466.

11. False Door: Egyptian Museum, Berlin. Accession number 73/71.

12. Tomb stela: Egyptian Museum, Berlin. Accession number 932.

Plates 1–4 and 10–12 are museum photographs; Plates 5–9 were photographs taken for the European Tutankhamun Exhibition, 1980–1981.